The Life of ABRAHAM LINCOLN

Books by STEFAN LORANT

I WAS HITLER'S PRISONER

LINCOLN; HIS LIFE IN PHOTOGRAPHS

THE NEW WORLD

FDR; A PICTORIAL BIOGRAPHY

THE PRESIDENCY

LINCOLN; A PICTURE STORY OF HIS LIFE

THE LIFE OF ABRAHAM LINCOLN

THE LIFE OF

ABRAHAM

A SHORT, ILLUSTRATI

McGRAW-HILL BOOK COMPANY, IN

LINCOLN

OGRAPHY *by Stefan Lorant*

W YORK TORONTO LONDON

THE LIFE OF ABRAHAM LINCOLN
A Short, Illustrated Biography

Library of Congress Catalog Card Number: 54–7674

Published by the McGraw-Hill Book Company, Inc.
Printed in the United States of America

For Edgar J. Kaufmann in friendship

Contents

PICTURE SECTIONS

Acknowledgments

No illustrated book on Abraham Lincoln could be published without the basic research of Frederick Hill Meserve, who, for more than half a century, assiduously collected Lincoln negatives and photographs. For his pioneering job he has the everlasting gratitude of all Lincoln students. The poignant broken plate portrait reproduced on page 135 is one of the rare items in his monumental photographic collection.

However, most of the Lincoln pictures in this volume were made directly from the original prints, ambrotypes and daguerreotypes, using the latest techniques of reproduction.

The list of librarians and owners of prints who generously assisted me is such a long one that I must thank them collectively, but I cannot refrain from singling out Mr. Emerson C. Ives, the grandson of the painter Francis B. Carpenter, who allowed me to make an enlargement of his small Brady negative, reproduced on page 130.

I am grateful to Dr. Harry E. Pratt of the Illinois State Historical Library and Dr. Louis A. Warren of the Lincoln National Life Foundation for their kind co-operation.

The coffin picture on page 136 is printed through the courtesy of the Illinois State Historical Library, where it was found not long ago by the fifteen-year-old Lincoln student Donald Rietveld.

My deeply felt thanks go to Mrs. Irene F. Weston,

who typed the manuscript and was a constant help with valuable suggestions and criticism.

The numbering of the Lincoln portraits follows my larger study, *Lincoln; A Picture Story of His Life*, in which volume I have listed all the known Lincoln photographs in chronological order.

STEFAN LORANT

As I would not be a slave, so I
would not be a master- This ex=
presses my idea of democracy—
Whatever differs from this, to the
extent of the difference, is no
democracy—

A. Lincoln-

Part One

1. *His Early Years*

A cabin in the Kentucky wilderness; eighteen feet wide, sixteen feet long. The floor, packed-down dirt; sparse light through a solitary window. Opposite the open hearth a bed of cornhusks and bearskins. There, on February 12, 1809, Abraham Lincoln first saw the life of this world.

The father of the newborn was a carpenter by trade; a stout, thickset man with a round face, swarthy complexion and black hair. Later, when books were written about his famous son, he was sketched as an ever moving, shiftless, good-for-nothing creature. But his record shows nothing of the kind. Thomas Lincoln was sober, hard-working, industrious, not a great success in life, but neither was he a failure. He owned hundreds of acres of land and he was never without a horse. A tax book in 1814 lists him fifteenth out of ninety-eight names in the valuation of property owners.

His forebears came from England. Samuel Lincoln, a weaver's apprentice, left the Old Country in 1637, settling in Hingham, Massachusetts. From there the Lincolns spread to New Jersey, Pennsylvania, Virginia, then westward along the Wilderness Road into Kentucky. And it was in that state that twenty-eight-year-old Thomas Lincoln married twenty-two-year-old Nancy Hanks on June 12, 1806.

Of Nancy Hanks little is known. A simple pioneer woman, who never learned to read or write, she will forever remain a shadowy figure. Her cousin described her as a woman of "remarkable keen perception," "shrewd and smart," "highly intellectual by nature," with a strong memory, accurate judgment, affectionate, religious, "spiritually and ideally inclined." Whether she was really all that, or whether she grew only in Dennis Hanks's memory to such a person, who can say? Her mother had become the wife of Henry Sparrow in 1791, years after Nancy's birth. There was much speculation as to Nancy's real father; Lincoln believed him "a well-bred Virginia planter." Others guessed differently.

After their marriage the Lincolns settled at Elizabethtown, where Thomas owned a house. Here their first child, Sarah, was born on February 10, 1807. Before long, he had saved up enough money to buy a 300 acre tract, for which he paid $200, all in cash. It was eighteen miles from Elizabethtown, (near the present Hodgenville), out in the open country, on Nolin Creek, where neighbors were sparse and life was lonely. To this place Thomas moved with his wife and daughter in the winter of 1808.

On the land stood a small log-cabin, built on a knoll near a spring, and it was here that Nancy expected her second child. Its arrival on a cold February morning was recalled by cousin Dennis, who eight decades later told an interviewer that he was present at the cabin not long after the baby's birth. "Nancy was lyin' thar in a pole bed lookin' purty happy," said Dennis. "Tom'd built up a good fire and throwed a b'ar skin over the kivers to keep 'em warm." Then Nancy's aunt came, washed the new born, "put a yaller flannen petticoat an' a linsey shirt on him, an' cooked some dried berries with wild honey for Nancy, an' slicked things up an' went home. An' that's all the nuss'n either of 'em got." It is a vivid description, and it may even be true.

The world into which the infant entered was no better or worse than the world usually is. It had war and it had peace, it had rich and poor, it had love and hate, it had happiness and misery. In the United States Thomas Jefferson was serving the end of his second term as President. Seventeen states belonged to the Union, and the population of the country was seven million two hundred thousand including the one million nine hundred thousand slaves. In Europe Great Britain was fighting France, trying to turn the tide against Napoleon. Hoping to remain neutral, the United States ceased to trade with the belligerents.

But the Lincolns cared little about politics. Thomas worked his land, and earned some extra money through carpentry; he shot game and he fished; Nancy took care of the cabin; she cooked and baked, washed and sewed and looked after the children.

The soil of the Nolin Creek farm proved barren, and Thomas bought another tract in a more thickly settled region on the old Cumberland Trail, the much-traveled road between Louisville and Nashville. There the family moved sometime in 1811. Lincoln later recalled his first memories of the Knob Creek home: "Our farm was composed of three fields which lay in the valley surrounded by high hills and deep gorges. Sometimes when there came a big rain in the hills the water would come down the gorges and spread over the farm. The last thing I remember of doing there was one Saturday afternoon; the other boys planted the corn in what we called the 'big field'—it contained seven acres—and I dropped the pumpkin seed. I dropped two seeds every other hill and every other row. The next Sunday morning there came a big rain in the hills; it did not rain a drop in the valley, but the water, coming down through the gorges, washed ground, corn, pumpkin seeds and all clear off the field."

It was a lovely spot for a child whether roaming in woods, wading in the creek, setting traps for rabbits and muskrats or going with father on coon hunts.

When Abraham reached the age of six he trudged up the road to pick up some "readin', writin', and cipher-in'" from a teacher. But he learned more from his surroundings than he did in school; from the deep hollows and ravines, from the cedar trees and the creek's clear waters, from the land, peaceful and tranquil, pristine as on the day of its creation.

For five years the family lived on the Knob Creek farm. Then, on a winter day in 1816, a year so cold that it was remembered as "eighteen-hundred-and-froze-to-death," the Lincolns set out for Indiana. Thomas, like other settlers in Kentucky, was plagued by title difficulties. Three times he had had to fight in the courts for the lands he had bought, lands he had worked and developed. Now he would go to a state with a government survey, where titles were safe and where land caused no trouble.

With the Lincolns went the Sparrows, Nancy's aunt and uncle, and Dennis Hanks, their foster son. They headed for the rich and fertile forest near Little Pigeon Creek, a mile and a half east of Gentryville.

"Tom brought his tools," remembered Dennis, "an' four hundred gallons o' whiskey to trade fur land with Mr. Gentry. It was in Spencer County, back a piece from the Ohio River. We had to chop down trees to make a road to the place, but it was good land, in the timber, whar the women could pick up their firewood, an' on a crick with a deer lick handy, an' a spring o' good water."

The new home was in "a wild region with many bears and other wild animals still in the woods." The families settled in an unbroken forest, and the clearing of surplus wood was the great task. They put in corn, wheat and oats, built a cabin and gradually became "reasonably comfortable."

In the long-handled frying pan Nancy roasted the game which Thomas shot, fried the salt pork and bacon; in the clay oven she baked bread. There was plenty to eat; wild turkey and chicken, and fish from the creek. In the summer she gathered wild berries and dried them; in the fall she picked apples and pumpkins. And in the long winter evenings she spun and wove, making woolen blankets and spinning linsey-woolsey for the children.

Two years went by—two years of work, two years of life with not much to remember. But the year of 1818 will never be forgotten—a dark year, full of tragedy. In the fall Thomas Sparrow and his wife came down with the milk-sickness and died. Then Nancy got ill, and she too passed away.

"Oh Lord, oh Lord, I'll never furgit it, the miz'ry in that cabin in the woods when Nancy died," recalled Dennis, the chronicler of those days. "Abe an' me helped Tom make the coffin. He tuk a log left over from makin' the cabin, and I helped him whipsaw it into planks an' plane 'em. Me an' Abe held the planks while Tom bored holes an' put 'em together with pegs Abe'd whittled."

It was a sad time that winter, a sad and hard and lonely time. Sarah took over the household duties, but she was only twelve.

Thomas needed a wife, the children needed a mother. So he went back to Elizabethtown to bespeak Sarah Bush, whom he had courted before he married Nancy Hanks.

Sarah Bush was then a widow. Her husband, Johnston, had died and left her with three children.

The scene between Thomas Lincoln and Sarah Bush Johnston was short.

"Well, Miss Johnston," said Thomas, "I have no wife, and you have no husband. I came a purpose to marry you. I knowed you from a gal, and you knowed me from a boy. I have no time to lose; and, if you are willin', let it be done straight off."

And Sarah replied:

"Tommy, I know you well, and have no objection to marrying you; but I cannot do it straight off, as I owe some debts that must first be paid."

"Give me a list of them," said Thomas, and he paid the debts that very evening. The next morning—on December 2, 1819—they were married.

A day later Thomas loaded Sarah's chest of drawers, her flax wheel, her cooking pots and pewter dishes, her soap kettle and all the household goods on a borrowed wagon, and set out with his new wife and her three children — twelve-year-old Elizabeth, eight-year-old Matilda, and five-year-old John—for Indiana.

What the new Mrs. Lincoln found at Pigeon Creek was not heart warming: a cabin without windows and floor, the children unkempt and dirty. She ordered Dennis to move the carpenter bench outside the door "near the hoss trough" and to fill the trough with spring water. And she put out a big gourd full of soft soap, another one to dip water with, and told them to wash up for dinner.

Thomas "put in a new floor he'd whipsawed an' planed off so she could scour it," then he "made some good beds an' cheers, an' tinkered at the roof so it couldn't snow in."

The three boys, Abraham Lincoln, Dennis Hanks and John Johnston, slept in the loft; Sarah Lincoln, the two Johnston girls, Thomas and his wife downstairs. The small single room of the cabin housed eight human beings.

Abraham Lincoln
his hand and pen .
he will be good but
god knows When

A VERSE from his exercise book, scribbled by the child Lincoln sometime between the years of 1824 and 1826.

Abraham loved his new mother and she was deeply fond of him. "He was the best boy I ever saw," said she in her old age. "I never gave him a cross word in all my life . . . His mind and mine, what little I had, seemed to run together, move in the same channel." And Lincoln said: "All that I am, or hope to be, I owe to my angel mother." She encouraged him to read. "Abe read all the books he could lay his hands on, and when he came across a passage that struck him, he would write it down on boards if he had no paper and keep it there till he did get paper, then he would rewrite it, look at it, repeat it." And she recalled that "Abe could easily learn and long remember, and when he did learn anything he learned it well and thoroughly."

He read Aesop's *Fables* and *Robinson Crusoe*, Weems' *Life of Washington*, Bunyan's *Pilgrim's Progress* and Grimshaw's *History of the United States*, and he was at home in the Bible. His stepsister remembered that "when father and mother would go to church, Abe would take down the Bible, read a verse, give out a hymn, and we would sing . . . He preached, and we would do the crying."

In his tenth year he was kicked by a frightened horse and knocked unconscious. It happened at the mill as he was driving the animal to furnish power for grinding some corn. He started to call out, "Come on, you old Hussy," but all he could say was, "Come on," when the horse kicked him. Next day, when he awoke he said "you old Hussy," finishing the sentence of the day before. This accident might have had influenced his later moodiness and melancholy.

He grew tall. Before he was seventeen he measured 6 feet 2 inches, and weighed about a hundred and sixty pounds. Hired out among the neighbors, wielding an ax, he split rails, cleared land. Those who knew him said that he was lazy, "always reading and thinking."

In the evenings he would walk to Gentryville, lingering in the grocery. He was a good entertainer, had a gift for imitating others and a talent for oratory. He could tell stories and make the fellows laugh like no one else.

In his nineteenth year he was hired by James Gentry to take a flatboat of produce to New Orleans. He and Gentry's son traded along the sugar coast and it was there they fought a gang of Negroes who attacked them.

At last they reached New Orleans, the first great city Lincoln had ever seen, a fascinating new world for the pioneer youth, a world of elegance and magic.

When Lincoln returned home, his father was once more in a moving mood. The farm in Indiana paid poorly, and once more the plague of milk-sickness threatened the cattle. John Hanks was living in Illinois, from where he sent glowing reports of the land, and Thomas had made up his mind to follow him.

By the middle of February he had disposed of his holdings for $125, sold his corn and hogs, piled all his belongings into ox wagons—all the bedding, furniture, ovens, skillets—and started on the slow, tedious and tiresome journey. The whole family moved together, thirteen in all. The Johnston girls were by then married, one to Dennis Hanks, the other to Squire Hall, the Hanks having four children, the Halls, one. Lincoln's sister Sarah was not with them; three years before, she had married Aaron Grigsby, a year later she died in childbirth.

After two hundred miles of travel, crossing icy creeks and rivers, the little group reached the bank of the Sangamon River about ten miles from Decatur. Here they built a cabin, made enough rails "to fence ten acres of ground, fenced and broke the ground, and raised a crop of sown corn upon it the same year."

The winter came hard; it snowed and it rained, and the rain froze and was snowed over again. Cows and horses broke through the crust. And when the "deep snow" went off, Abraham left home, to paddle down

FLOATING DOWN THE MISSISSIPPI. In 1828 and again in 1831 young Lincoln took some produce to New Orleans.

the Sangamon with John Hanks and his stepbrother, John Johnston. They were hired by Denton Offutt, a colorful man of the frontier, to take produce to New Orleans. They found Offutt near Springfield, but no boat. So they cut timber, sawed it into logs, made one, loaded it with barrels of pork and corn and live hogs and then started off.

Offutt, who at the beginning of the trip was with them, "conceived a liking for Abraham, and believing he could turn him to account, he contracted with him to act as clerk for him, on his return from New Orleans, in charge of a store and mill at New Salem."

In July 1831 Lincoln arrived at New Salem. He was twenty-two years old; he had come of age and was on his own. But—so he later said—"I did not know much. Still, somehow, I could read, write, and cipher to the Rule of Three, but that was all. I was never in college or academy as a student. What I have in the way of education I have picked up from time to time under pressure of necessity."

To a clergyman who was wondering how he got "this unusual power of putting things . . . it must have been a matter of education," Lincoln replied thoughtfully, "No man has it by nature alone." Then he elaborated: "I never went to school more than twelve months in my life. But as you say, this must be a product of culture in *some* form. . . . Among my earliest recollections, I remember how, when a mere child, I used to get irritated when anybody talked to me in a way I could not understand. I don't think I ever got angry at anything else in my life. But that always disturbed my temper, and has ever since. I can remember going to my little bedroom, after hearing the neighbors talk, of an evening, with my father, and spending no small part of the night walking up and down, and trying to make out what was the exact meaning of some of their, to me, dark sayings. I could not sleep, though I often tried to, when I got on such a hunt after an idea, until I had caught it; and when I thought I had got it, I was not satisfied until I had repeated it over and over, until I had put it in language plain enough, as I thought, for any boy I knew to comprehend. This was a kind of passion with me, and it has stuck by me, for I am never easy now, when I am handling a thought, till I have bounded it north and bounded it south, and bounded it east, and bounded it west."

At the time he was running for the Presidency and a newspaper man asked him about his childhood days, Lincoln said that it would be a great piece of folly to attempt to make anything out of him or his early life. "It can all be condensed into a single sentence, and that sentence you will find in Grey's 'Elegy'—the short and simple annals of the poor. That's my life, and that's all you or anyone else can make out of it."

2. Earning a Living

When he came to stop "indefinitely and for the first time, as it were, by himself at New Salem," only a handful of families lived there. It was a small community and it never did grow to be large. In its heyday the village housed no more than a hundred people.

The lanky young man sauntered around, got acquainted, and when Denton Offutt arrived with the merchandise, the store was opened.

It was like others of the frontier: furs, mittens, hides, pots, plates and glassware filled shelves; sugar, salt and coffee, imported through St. Louis, were on the counters; firearms, saddles, ox yokes and tools cluttered the walls and the corners.

Situated on the bluff above the Sangamon River and near the mill, it was next to the saloon of Bill Clary,

17

whose brother founded the Clary's Grove settlement, the home of a crowd of reckless, hard-drinking, hard-fighting young men. The leader of them was Jack Armstrong, the strongest of them all.

But for Denton Offutt no one could be stronger than his clerk, who—so he boasted—could throw any man in the neighborhood. To prove that it was not so, Jack Armstrong challenged Lincoln to a wrestling match—a most celebrated event of the village. Neither man could throw the other, but from then on Lincoln had the respect of the boys.

The hours in the store passed pleasantly. If a customer came, he lingered for a talk, and when the store was empty, Lincoln read and studied. He made friends with Mentor Graham, the teacher, who taught him mathematics and encouraged him to take up grammar. Another villager, the easy-going Jack Kelso, read poetry to him, introducing him to the magic of Shakespeare and Robert Burns.

With the coming of spring, "encouraged by his great popularity among his immediate neighbors," Lincoln decided to run for the State Legislature. In a circular he announced his candidacy and set forth his policies, advocating internal improvements, aids to education and laws against usury. "Every man is said to have his peculiar ambition," read the closing lines of his platform, "whether it be true or not, I can say for one that I have no other so great as that of being truly esteemed of my fellow men, by rendering myself worthy of their esteem. How far I shall succeed in gratifying this ambition, is yet to be developed. I am young and unknown to many of you. I was born and have ever remained in the most humble walks of life. I have no wealthy or popular relations to recommend me. My case is thrown exclusively upon the independent voters of this county, and if elected they will have conferred a favor upon me, for which I shall be unremitting in my labors to compensate. But if the good people in their wisdom shall see fit to keep me in the background, I have been too familiar with disappointments to be very much chagrined."

The chief interest of the villagers was the navigation of their river. If the Sangamon could be used by large boats, they could receive cheaper goods. News came about the steamer *Talisman*, ready to "deliver freight from St. Louis at the landing on the Sangamon River, opposite the town of Springfield, for thirty-seven and a half cents for 100 pounds"—less than half the overland charge. Its captain hired some men with long-handled axes to go before the boat and cut off overhanging limbs and clear the obstructions from the river. Lincoln was one of them.

But when the *Talisman* began its return voyage, the Sangamon was so shallow that the boat—with Lincoln as one of its pilots—could be kept barely under way; at New Salem part of the dam had to be torn down.

The excitement about the *Talisman* had hardly spent itself when New Salem heard that Black Hawk, an Indian chief, had recrossed the border of Illinois and was spreading terror along the frontier. Lincoln responded to the governor's call for a thousand mounted volunteers, and was chosen captain by the men of his company.

Of military matters Captain Lincoln knew nothing. At one time when his men reached a narrow gate and he could not remember the right command, he ordered: "Halt! This company will break ranks for two minutes and form again on the other side of the gate."

His thirty-day enlistment over, he reenlisted; altogether he spent three months in the war, receiving $125 for his services. He saw no action, he was not in any fighting. But he made friends, learned new stories, saw more of the land.

Returning to New Salem, he resumed his campaign for the Legislature. At Pappsville he addressed a crowd, looking odd in his short flax and tow-linen pantaloons, calico shirt, blue yarn socks and straw hat. When a fight broke out in the audience he left his platform, seized the man who had started the melee by the neck and the seat of his trousers, and threw him twelve feet away. Then he continued: "My politics are short and sweet, like the old woman's dance. I am in favor of a national bank. I am in favor of the internal improvement system and a high protective tariff. These are my sentiments and political principles. If elected I shall be thankful; if not, it will be all the same."

He was not elected, the only time—so he recalled—that he "was ever beaten on a direct vote of the people." And to make matters worse the Offutt store folded and he found himself without a job. He " thought of learning the blacksmith trade—thought of trying to

I CERTIFY, That *David M Pantier* volunteered and served *of a private* in the Company of Mounted Volunteers under my command, in the Regiment commanded by Col. SAMUEL M. THOMPSON, in the Brigade under the command of Generals S. WHITESIDE and H. ATKINSON, called into the service of the United States by the Commander-in-Chief of the Militia of the State, for the protection of the North Western Frontier against an Invasion of the British Band of Sac and other tribes of Indians,—that he was enrolled on the *21st* day of *April* 1832, and was HONORABLY DISCHARGED on the *7th* day of *June* thereafter, having served *48 days*

Given under my hand. this *26th* day of *September* 1832.
A Lincoln Capt.

CAPTAIN LINCOLN CERTIFIES that a volunteer served under his command in the war against Indian Chief Black Hawk in 1832. Lincoln himself enlisted as militiaman on April 21 and was mustered out July 16, without seeing battle.

Mr Spears

At your request. I send you a receipt for the postage on your paper — I am some what surprised at your request. I will however comply with it — The law requires News paper postage to be paid in advance and now that I have waited a free year you choose to wound my feelings by insinuating that unless you get a receipt I will probably make you pay it again —

Respectfully
A. Lincoln

Received of George Spears in full for postage on the Sangamo Journal up to the first of July 1834

A. Lincoln P M

POSTMASTER LINCOLN of New Salem wrote this receipt for George Spears: "The law requires News paper postage to be paid in advance and now that I have waited a full year you choose to wound my feelings by insinuating that unless you get a receipt I will probably make you pay it again."

study law—rather thought he could not succeed at that without a better education."

He and another young man bought a stock of goods for a little cash, but mostly on credit, and thus the Berry-Lincoln store came into being. But their dream lasted only for a short while. The two storekeepers went deeper and deeper in debt, and when "the store winked out," Lincoln owed about eleven hundred dollars.

Through the help of friends he was appointed postmaster of New Salem, "the office being too insignificant to make his politics an objection." He held the office for the next three years, earning on the average about a dollar a week. His task was to estimate the number of pages in the letters—stamps and envelopes were not yet in use—figure out the mileage, and mark the fee in the corner. That he was not too businesslike we gather from a letter of a villager who informed his brother: "The Post Master is very careless about leaving his office open and unlocked during the day—half the time I go in and get my papers, etc. without anyone being there . . ."

To supplement his meager income he split rails, helped at a mill, gave a hand at harvesting, tended store for Sam Hill, and took whatever came his way. When the county surveyor was willing to make him his assistant, he threw himself into studying Flint's *Treatise on Geometry, Trigonometry and Rectangular Surveying,* bought a compass and chain, also a horse and a saddle on credit.

For establishing a quarter-section of land he received about two and a half dollars, for traveling he charged about two dollars a day. As he later noted in his autobiographical sketch: "This procured bread, and kept soul and body together."

For one of his first surveys he was paid with two buckskins, which Hannah Armstrong, the wife of Jack, "foxed" on his pants to protect them from briars.

In the spring of 1834 he tried again for the Legislature, and this time was elected. During the campaign Major John Todd Stuart, one of the Whig leaders in the state, encouraged him to become a lawyer. Lincoln borrowed books from him "and went at it in good earnest. He studied with nobody. He still mixed in the surveying to pay board and clothing bills."

In the fall of that year the twenty-five-year-old legislator bought himself a new suit to present himself at Vandalia, the capital of Illinois.

ONE OF LINCOLN'S FIRST SURVEYS. Towards the end of the year 1833 he bought a compass and chain on credit and became a deputy of John Calhoun, the county surveyor. He said: "This procured bread, and kept soul and body together."

Five days after the opening of the session he addressed the Assembly, proposing a bill "to limit the jurisdiction of Justices of Peace"; later he offered other bills, like the one about a toll bridge across Salt Creek, or about marking and locating a road from Springfield to Miller's Ferry.

In this session the Legislature debated two great measures: the construction of the Illinois and Michigan Canal, and the charter of a state bank. Both proposals were passed, Lincoln casting his vote with the majority.

In Vandalia, Lincoln learned the art of politics. With eyes and ears open he observed and watched; he made friends and learned about people. Every time the Legislature recessed, he returned to New Salem, took over the work in the post office, continued with his surveys, studied law.

In 1836 he was re-elected as one of the nine Whigs from Sangamon County, all so tall that they were called the "Long Nine." He also passed the bar examination, and on September 9, 1836, he was licensed to practice law.

The Tenth General Assembly of Illinois, which con-

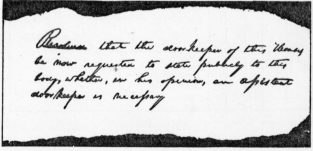

LEGISLATOR LINCOLN'S resolution at Vandalia, asking the doorkeeper of the House "to state publicly to this body, whether, in his opinion, an assistant doorkeeper is necessary."

HIS BIRTHPLACE. The log cabin on Nolin Creek in Kentucky, near present-day Hodgenville, where Abraham Lincoln was born on February 12, 1809. His father bought the 300-acre tract with the cabin on it for $200.

THE BIRTHDAY CABIN from the outside and inside. T
reconstructed interior of the Chicago Historical Socie
views the room from the bed where Lincoln was bor

THE LINCOLN HOME AT KNOB CREEK, KY., near the much-traveled road from Louisville to Nashville, to which the family moved in 1811 and where it stayed for 5 years.

LINCOLN'S FIRST HOME IN ILLINOIS. After living fourteen years in Indiana the Lincolns moved in 1830 to Illinois, where Thomas, helped by his son, built this cabin.

THE RUTLEDGE TAVERN in New Salem, where Lincol▌
boarded for a while. According to a deep-rooted legend, h▌
fell in love with Ann Rutledge, the daughter of the hous▌

THE LEAN-TO of the Berry-Lincoln store in New Sale▌
served as his sleeping quarters. After the store "winke▌
out," Lincoln became the postmaster of the villag▌

THE OFFUTT STORE in New Salem, where Lincoln worked as a clerk, was situated on the bluff above the Sangamon River, not far from the "grocery" of Bill Clary.

LINCOLN'S FIRST LAW OFFICE in Springfield, Ill., whe
he was the partner of John Todd Stuart. Below, his last lav
office, the one which housed the firm of Lincoln & Herndor

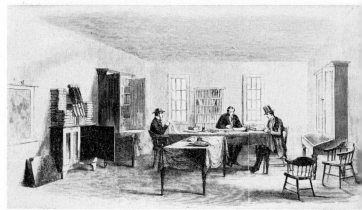

THE GLOBE TAVERN IN SPRINGFIELD. Here for $4 week the newly-wed Lincolns received room and board
Here on August 1, 1843, their first child was born

HIS HOME IN SPRINGFIELD. Lincoln bought the one-and-a-half story cottage a year after his marriage for $1500. Here his other boys—Eddie, Willie and Tad—were born.

THE INSIDE OF THE SPRINGFIELD HOME at Eighth and Jackson Streets. The front parlor and (below) the sitting room as they looked at the time of Lincoln's election.

Lorant No. 88

LINCOLN'S HOME IN SPRINGFIELD after it was enlarged into a two-story building. Behind the railing Lincoln is posing with one of his sons for photographer A. J. Whipple.

THE WHITE HOUSE IN WASHINGTON, Abraham Lincoln's residence for four critical years—from his inauguration on March 4, 1861, till his assassination on April 14, 1865.

vened in December 1836, turned out to be one of the most remarkable in Illinois history. It passed a record number of bills, legislating aids to an enormous internal improvement system. Lincoln took an active part in the debates; he was already a resourceful parliamentarian, a shrewd practitioner of log rolling, with a burning ambition to become the "DeWitt Clinton of Illinois."

As Vandalia was in the southern part of the State, and as population was pushing northward, Lincoln and his friends from Sangamon advocated the relocation of the capital to Springfield. The "Long Nine," under his leadership, "threw itself as a unit in support of, or opposition to, every local measure of interest, but never without a bargain for votes in return on the seat of government question."

The budget of Illinois showed a surplus of about two and three-quarter million dollars, which was to be allocated for railroads, canals, turnpikes and the like. As all legislators desired to have some of the appropriations for their own communities, the position of the "Long Nine" in their battle for Springfield as capital was strong. With their nine votes Lincoln bargained

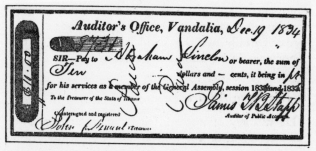

A SALARY WARRANT for Lincoln's services as legislator in the Illinois General Assembly. During his four terms he received $1762 as salary and $188 for travel expense.

cleverly. By promising to support a canal here and a road there, he received assurances for the relocation of the capital.

It was during this session that Lincoln, with his colleague Dan Stone, declared that the institution of slavery was "founded on both injustice and bad policy" and "that the Congress of the United States has no power under the Constitution to interfere with the institution of slavery in the different states."

Twenty-three years later, when he was running for the Presidency, he reiterated that his position on the slavery question "so far as it goes . . . was then the same that it is now."

To evaluate Lincoln's years in Vandalia one could do no better than to quote the words of Professor Baringer: "In the muddy village of Vandalia he learned and practiced the subtleties of his trade under the example and tutelage of experienced politicians. Here for the first time he mingled in polite society with men and women of wealth, culture, education; here he debated and heard discussed every phase of national and state politics and economic theory, probing problems of slavery and abolition, banking, states' rights, executive powers and patronage, temperance, internal improvements, public lands, tariff education, capital punishment, judicial procedure, financial panic. As a formative influence the Vandalia period was of first importance in his astonishing career."

3. *His Love Affairs*

He was shy of women, felt far more at ease in the company of men. Yet women held a great fascination for him.

The story of his love for Ann Rutledge is part of our folklore. Billy Herndon gave a lecture in which he exclaimed that Lincoln "loved Ann Rutledge better than his own life," that he loved her "with all his soul, mind and strength." And when twenty-three-year-old Ann died, he "slept not . . . ate not, joyed not," but "his mind wandered from its throne . . . walked out of itself along the uncolumned air, and kissed and embraced the shadows and illusions of the heated brain."

Herndon based these allegations on the flimsiest evidence, on hearsay, gossip and the remembrance of old people. At the time of the lecture Lincoln had been in his grave over a year; he could not contradict. But Mary Lincoln protested hotly: "I shall assuredly remain firm in my conviction that Ann Rutledge is a myth." Her husband could not have loved Ann, as he "was *truth itself*, and he has always assured me, he had cared for no one but myself." During their twenty-two years of married life she had never heard him speak of Ann Rutledge. "In all his confidential communications, such a romantic name was never breathed. . . . Nor did his life or his joyous laugh lead one to suppose his heart was in any unfortunate woman's grave—but in the proper place with his loved wife and children."

Still, Herndon's romantic tale caught the imagination; Ann Rutledge became the legendary sweetheart of Abraham Lincoln. Her name is known by everyone, but who knows the name of Mary Owens? Who knows the name of the girl whom Lincoln was courting and asked to marry, only a year after Ann Rutledge's death?

Mary Owens, a year older than her suitor, had "fair skin, deep blue eyes, and dark curling hair; height five feet, five inches; weight about a hundred and fifty pounds." She met Lincoln in New Salem, where she visited her married sister. They seemed to grow fond of each other, took part in quilting bees and outings.

And when Lincoln left for the Legislature he sent her a note from Vandalia: "Write back as soon as you get this, and, if possible, say something that will please me, for really I have not been pleased since I left you."

And we have another letter written a year later, when he was already living in Springfield.

"I am often thinking of what we said about your coming to Springfield. I am afraid you would not be satisfied. There is a great deal of flourishing about in carriages here, which it would be your doom to see without sharing it. You would have to be poor, without the means of hiding your poverty. Do you believe you could bear that patiently? Whatever woman may cast her lot with mine, should any ever do so, it is my intention to do all in my power to make her happy and contented; and there is nothing I can imagine that would make me more unhappy than to fail in the effort. I know I should be much happier with you than the way I am, provided I saw no signs of discontent in you. What you have said to me may have been in the way of jest, or I may have misunderstood it. If so, then let it be forgotten; if otherwise, I much wish you would think seriously before you decide. What I have said I will most positively abide by, provided you wish it. My opinion is that you had better not do it. You have not been accustomed to hardship, and it may be more severe than you now imagine. I know you are capable of thinking correctly on any subject, and if you deliberate maturely upon this before you decide, then I am willing to abide your decision."

Mary Owens was not willing to become his wife. She had her reasons. Once when they were riding with friends, the party came to a treacherous stream. All the men helped their ladies to cross safely—all but Lincoln, who rode on, never even looking back. "I suppose you did not care, whether my neck was broken or not," chided Mary, and he replied that she was plenty smart enough to take care of herself.

There were other such incidents. Like the one when a friend of theirs was carrying her child up a hill, panting and sweating, and he would not offer his hand. Mary might have thought: Would this be so with her after she married him? Would he go his way, leaving things to her?

Once, Lincoln journeyed to New Salem to see her. And the very day he returned to Springfield, he penned her this note:

"You will no doubt think it rather strange that I should write you a letter on the same day on which we parted, and I can only account for it by supposing that seeing you lately makes me think of you more than usual." He asserted: "I want at this particular time, more than anything else, to do right with you; and if I knew it would be doing right, as I rather suspect it would, to let you alone, I would do it. . . ." Doubts and uncertainty racked his mind. He was fond of Mary, he desired to marry her, and yet he hesitated. "If you feel yourself in any degree bound to me, I am now willing to release you, provided you wish it; while on the other hand, I am willing and even anxious to bind you faster, if I can be convinced that it will, in any considerable degree, add to your happiness."

But Mary Owens had no wish to become Lincoln's wife. Some thirty years later when she was asked why she had refused, she said: "Mr. Lincoln was deficient in those little links which make up the chain of woman's happiness—at least it was so in my case."

And Lincoln? After Mary refused him, he unburdened himself to a friend, trying "to give a full and intelligible account of the things I have done and suffered."

In his strangely unchivalrous letter to Mrs. Browning

he speaks of Mary Owens as "over-size . . . a fair match for Falstaff. . . . I could not for my life avoid thinking of my mother; and this not for withered features—for her skin was too full of fat to permit of its contracting into wrinkles—but from her want of teeth, and weatherbeaten appearance in general." What a description of the woman whom only a few months earlier he wanted to make his wife.

In his letter Lincoln revealed that he had made her a proposal, "but shocking to relate, she answered, No." He asked her again, and again her answer was no. And when he realized that Mary's rejection was final, "I was mortified, it seemed to me, in a hundred different ways. My vanity was deeply wounded by the reflections, that I had so long been too stupid to discover her intentions, and at the same time never doubting that I understood them perfectly; and also, that she whom I had taught myself to believe nobody else would have, had actually rejected me with all my fancied greatness; and to cap the whole, I then, for the first time, began to suspect that I was really a little in love with her. But let it all go. I'll try and outlive it. Others have been made fools of by the girls; but this can never with truth be said of me. I most emphatically, in this instance, made a fool of myself. I have now come to the conclusion never again to think of marrying, and for this reason; I can never be satisfied with anyone who would be blockhead enough to have me."

The only excuse for such an epistle was that it bore the date of April 1, 1838—an April Fool's Day.

4. *Legislator*

In the middle of March, 1837, the Legislature adjourned and Lincoln returned to New Salem. But the days of the village were numbered—one by one the

LAWYER LINCOLN. An advertisement in the *Sangamo Journal* announcing his partnership with John T. Stuart.

settlers moved away. The post office had already been transferred to nearby Petersburg; a little while more and New Salem would be abandoned.

Lincoln, too, was ready to turn his back on the place where he lived for almost six years, and where he grew from an uncouth youth to an accomplished politician. On April 15 he left New Salem and rode to Springfield, all his earthly belongings in his saddlebags. He was twenty-eight years old, and he had twenty-eight years more to live—to the very day.

His first need was a bed; so he walked into the store of Joshua Speed to buy one. But when the merchant figured that it would come to $17, Lincoln's face darkened and he said, "It is probably cheap enough; but I want to say that cheap as it is, I have not the money to pay. But if you will credit me until Christmas, and my experiment here as a lawyer is a success, I will pay you then. If I fail in that I will probably never pay you at all."

Speed felt pity for the young lawyer and came up with a suggestion: "As so small a debt seems to affect you so deeply, I think I can suggest a plan by which you will be able to attain your end without incurring any debt. I have a very large room and a very large double bed in it, which you are perfectly welcome to share with me if you choose." Lincoln raced up the stairs, looked over the room, and when he came down he said all pleasure and smiles: "Well, Speed, I am moved."

At first he felt strange in the new city. "I am quite as lonesome here as I ever was anywhere in my life," he complained to Mary Owens. But soon he was immersed in law cases, as the junior partner of John Todd Stuart, and occupied with political matters. In an anonymous letter to the *Sangamo Journal* he charged the Democratic candidate for probate judge, General James Adams, with dishonesty and fraud. The letter showed Lincoln for what he then was, a rough-hewn politician with ethics to match. If Adams was guilty of dishonesty, the place to try him was not in newspaper columns, but in the courts.

His law practice prospered, his political career flourished. In 1838 he was re-elected to the Legislature; in the summer of 1839 he became trustee of Springfield; and in 1840 he was chosen for the fourth consecutive term as a legislator. In that year he was made presidential elector in the first Whig state convention, which selected General William Henry Harrison.

Why did a man with Lincoln's background join the Whigs, the party of the well-to-do, the party of the bankers and businessmen? Why wasn't he behind Andrew Jackson, who fought for more democracy and for improved conditions for the common man? Lincoln

40

respected tradition; he believed in the existing economic order. Let Jackson attack the banks and monopolies; his "beau ideal of a statesman" was Henry Clay. He admired Clay's policies, his "American System," which asked a protective tariff for the budding industries, advocated the development of the country's resources, proposed internal improvements and demanded a stable currency.

If fate had taken Lincoln in the early years of the eighteen forties, no one would know of him today. He was an obscure politician who proposed bills more often than not for the personal benefit of his constituents.

But his four terms in the Legislature taught him a great deal. He learned how to argue and how to compromise, when to be unbending and when to be soft. During these years his horizon widened; he became aware that politics was an art of give and take; and he learned to know people and to understand their problems. His later greatness was built on this foundation.

5. *Mary Todd*

She was not like the girls he had known before. Vivacious, temperamental, attractive, Mary Todd came from a wealthy family, had a good education, spoke French fluently, was well versed in literature and music. A sister of Mrs. Ninian W. Edwards, who had married the governor's son, she came to Springfield to look for a husband.

They first met in the winter of 1839 at a ball which celebrated the removal of the Illinois capital from Vandalia to Springfield. As she stood in the ballroom, dressed in silk, with neck and shoulders bare, Lincoln came up to her: "Miss Todd, I want to dance with you the worst way." And, as Mary later recalled, "he certainly did."

From that evening on they were steady companions. They read books together and poetry, and they discussed politics. Mary's sister, in whose house they met, recalled that it was mostly Mary who led the conversation. "Mr. Lincoln would sit at her side and listen. He scarcely said a word, but gazed on her as if irresistibly drawn toward her by some superior and unseen power."

And a niece of hers recorded: "Mary had been as fascinated with Mr. Lincoln's personality from their very first meeting as he had been with her grace and wit. Each found in the other the novelty which is most winsome to lovers. He found in her a bubbling fun, an enthusiastic love of life. She in turn was intrigued by his moodiness, his sincerity and honesty, his freedom from the pretty flatteries and the conventional gallantries of the men in her social set. He had never met a woman like Mary Todd, suave, equal to any social emergency. She had found for the first time a young man with a mentality dominating yet in accord with her own."

During the winter months their feelings deepened, and with the coming of spring Mary's mind was made up. She would neither be the wife of Stephen A. Douglas nor James Shields—two young politicians who had been courting her—but would become Mrs. Abraham Lincoln.

Her sisters were taken aback. They "showered her with advice and objections." For them Lincoln was not the right choice. He had no education and no money. Mary could do far better than to become his wife. But Mary did not waver in her decision.

It was Lincoln who became uneasy. Instead of being happy, he fell into one of his melancholy moods. The prospect of bondage filled him with dark premonitions. He saw a variety of reasons why a marriage between them would not work out. He tortured himself with morbid thoughts. And he wrote a note to Mary confessing that his love for her was not deep enough to warrant their union. But when he showed the letter to his roommate, Speed advised him not to send it.

"If you have the courage of manhood," Joshua Speed told him, "go see Mary yourself, tell her, if you do not love her, the facts, and that you will not marry her; but be quick about it, say little and leave soon."

Lincoln followed his friend's advice. He saw Mary and told her of his resolution. When the unhappy girl burst into tears Lincoln caught her in his arms, and instead of breaking the engagement, he renewed it. "Well, if I am in again, so be it. It's done, and I shall abide by it," he told Speed that night.

They quarreled, and made up, and quarreled again. Mary's outbursts drove him at times into despondency. On New Year's Day, 1841, they had another of their fights and parted—this time "forever." In his biography William Herndon perpetrated the legend that the wedding was set for that day, cakes baked, guests assembled, everything ready for the ceremony except the bridegroom, who "failed to appear!" Herndon's description, fixed in the minds of generations of Americans, is a romantic one but entirely untrue.

Why they broke off their relationship we do not know. Three weeks later Lincoln wrote to his law partner Stuart: "I am now the most miserable man living. If what I feel were equally distributed to the whole human family, there would not be one cheerful face on earth. Whether I shall ever be better I can not tell; I awfully forbode I shall not. To remain as I am is impossible; I must die or be better, it appears to me."

Those who observed him at that time said that he "went crazy as a loon." His friend James C. Conkling wrote about him that "he was confined a week, but though he now appears again he is reduced and emaciated in appearance and seems scarcely to possess the strength to speak above a whisper. His case at present is truly deplorable but what prospect there may be for ultimate relief I can not pretend to say. I doubt not but he can declare 'That loving is a painful thrill. And not to love more painful still!' "

In his despondent mood Lincoln turned to Dr. Drake, a well-known doctor in Cincinnati and asked him for advice. And when Dr. Drake—who presumably told him that he could not treat him by mail—was no help, Lincoln went to Dr. Anson G. Henry in Springfield, who suggested that old remedy for heartbroken lovers—a change of scenery.

Lincoln asked his law partner, who was then serving a term in Congress, to secure for him a consular post in South America. Stuart tried, but failed. So, instead of going to Bogota, Lincoln went to visit his friend Joshua Speed, whose family owned a farm outside Louisville.

He arrived at Farmington in low spirits. Dark thoughts of suicide tormented him. He felt that he had "done nothing to make any human being remember that he had lived; and that to connect his name with the events transpiring in his day and generation, and so impress himself upon them as to link his name with something that would redound to the interest of his fellowmen, was what he desired to live for."

Mary, too, was sad. To her friend she wrote: "After my gay companions of last winter departed, I was left much to the solitude of my own thoughts, and some *lingering regrets* over the past, which time can alone overshadow with its healing balm."

A year went by after they parted. Now Joshua Speed was in a similar state of mind to that of his friend the year before. Racked with uncertainty, he left Spring-

field for Louisville, pondering whether or not he
should marry. Lincoln urged him to make Fanny Hen-
ning his wife. And when, after some hesitation, Speed
made his decision, Lincoln wrote him:

"I incline to think it probable, that your nerves will
fail you occasionally for a while; but once you get
them fairly graded now, that trouble is over forever.
... If you went through the ceremony *calmly*, or even
with sufficient composure not to excite alarm in any
present, you are safe, beyond question; and in two or
three months, to say the most, will be the happiest of
men." A fortnight later he reassured Speed once more
that "our *forebodings*, for which you and I are rather
peculiar, are all the worst sort of nonsense."

Speed's marriage turned out well; this gave Lincoln
"more pleasure, than the total sums of all I have enjoyed since that fatal first of Jany." His thoughts were
still circling around Mary, whom he could not put out
of his mind. Speed advised him either to make her his
wife or to forget her. To this Lincoln replied:

"But before I resolve to do the one thing or the
other, I must regain my confidence in my own ability
to keep my resolves when they are made. In that ability, you know, I once prided myself as the only, or
at least the chief gem of my character; that gem I lost
—how, and when, you too well know. I have not yet
regained it; and until I do, I can not trust myself in any
matter of such importance."

And then it happened that he met her again. Springfield was too small a place to avoid each other. They
began to meet secretly, and together with Julia Jayne
they composed anonymous political letters attacking
James Shields, the Democratic State Auditor.

Shields demanded the name of the anonymous letter
writer, and the editor of the *Sangamo Journal* named
Lincoln. Shields asked for satisfaction, a duel was ar-

ranged, and stopped only at the last moment. Lincoln was ashamed of the affair; it taught him a lesson. Never again, as long as he lived, did he write another anonymous letter.

In the Fall of 1842 he wrote to Speed again, asking him "an impudent question." He wanted to know: "Are you now in *feeling* as well as *judgment*, glad you are married as you are?" Speed's answer must have been reassuring, for one early morning in November Lincoln knocked at James Matheny's door and asked him to be his best man, for he was going to marry that very night.

A few days later the benedict added to a business letter the sentence:

"Nothing new here, except my marrying, which to me, is a matter of profound wonder."

HIS MARRIAGE CERTIFICATE, given on November 4, 1842, by the Rev. Dresser, who performed the ceremony.

6. *Lawyer and Politician*

He had three law partnerships: with John T. Stuart from 1837 till 1841; with Stephen T. Logan from 1841 till 1844, and with William H. Herndon thereafter. No three men had greater influence on his life than they.

Mary Todd's cousin, John Todd Stuart, the socially prominent Whig leader in Springfield and their elected representative to Congress, encouraged him to practice law; took him under his wing, and asked to become a junior partner in his law firm, one of the busiest in Springfield.

When they parted, Lincoln became the associate of Judge Stephen T. Logan, whose mind was as orderly as his garments were not. Logan, ten years older than his junior partner, was a methodical and painstaking jurist, who instilled in Lincoln the importance of careful preparation and taught him to abandon sloppy habits of thinking.

When the partnership with Logan was dissolved, Lincoln turned to twenty-six-year-old William H. Herndon: "Billy, I can trust you, if you can trust me." Thus the firm Lincoln & Herndon came into being.

In every way Herndon was the opposite of his senior partner. While he was hot-blooded and radical, Lincoln was cautious and conservative. Herndon had no humor, Lincoln was full of it. Herndon loved liquor, Lincoln advocated temperance. But they never had an angry word for each other. Billy never wavered in his loyalty. For him Mr. Lincoln—as he always called him—could do no wrong.

Their office was ill-kept; neither partner was tidy. Windows were seldom washed, papers covered all the desks. They had no filing system. Lincoln stuck letters in his hat, Herndon took notes and papers home. On

47

a large envelope full of papers the senior partner wrote:

When you can't find it anywhere else look into this

The Springfield courts were in session only a few weeks each year. To make ends meet, lawyers had to ride the circuit. Lincoln travelled over the Eighth Judicial Circuit of Illinois, a vast territory of 12,000 square miles. Courts were held in hamlets, and between them lay wide open spaces. At times judges and lawyers had to be in the saddle or in a ramshackle carriage for thirty or more miles a day, rain drenching them to the bone, wind chilling them to the marrow.

Lincoln loved the law, but he loved politics more. In riding the circuit he learned how people's minds worked, what they thought and why they thought as they did. He mixed with them, won their affection and gained their support.

His political ambitions burned bright. He aimed to become a Congressman. To a friend he wrote in 1843: "Now, if you should hear anyone say that Lincoln don't want to go to Congress, I wish you, as a personal friend of mine, would tell him that you have reason to believe him mistaken. The truth is, I would like to go very much."

Yet, when the Whigs of the Seventh Congressional District had to choose among three candidates—Lincoln, Hardin and Baker—it was Edward Dickinson Baker whom they selected. Lincoln believed that he was defeated because he had been "put down as a candidate of pride, wealth and arristocratic [sic] family distinction" and because he "belonged to no church,

IN THE ACCOUNT BOOK of the firm Stuart & Lincoln the fees were entered by the junior partner. One of the entries shows a deduction of $15 for "credit by coat to Stuart."

was suspected of being a deist, and had talked about fighting a duel."

Sent as a delegate to the district's convention to propose Baker's candidacy, he felt "like a fellow who made a groomsman to a man that has cut him out and is marrying his own dear 'gal'." The district convention, however, did not endorse Baker, but John J. Hardin, so Lincoln advanced the motion that in the next election, two years away, Baker should become the choice of the party. It was a foresighted move, making it a principle that the candidates should rotate.

Hardin was succeeded by Baker, and when Baker returned from Washington in the summer of 1845, Lincoln exacted from him the promise to stand aside in the next election and let him have his turn. Baker was willing, but Hardin, who wanted the nomination himself, was not. Lincoln wrote him:

"If I am not (in services done the party and in capacity to serve in future) near enough your equal, when added to the fact of your having had a turn, to entitle me to the nomination, I scorn it on any and all grounds."

Steadfastly and shrewdly he rallied enough political support to force Hardin's withdrawal. And when Hardin was forced out of the race, the district convention nominated Lincoln.

The ensuing campaign was hard fought. His Democratic opponent was the well-known Methodist preacher Peter Cartwright. There is a story that during the canvass Lincoln walked into a religious meeting conducted by Cartwright, who after a hell-raising sermon called out: "All who desire to lead a new life, to give their hearts to God, and to go to heaven, will stand." A few in the congregation got to their feet. Cartwright thundered: "All who do not wish to go to hell will stand." The rest of the men and women rose —all but Lincoln. Cartwright turned his wrath on him: "May I inquire of you, Mr. Lincoln, where you are going?" Whereupon Lincoln is supposed to have answered in his slow, drawling way: "If it is all the same to you—I am going to Congress."

The Democrats made such an issue of Lincoln's infidelity that the accused candidate felt compelled to answer their charge in public. In a handbill he wrote:

"A charge having got into circulation in some of the neighborhoods of this District, in substance that I am an open scoffer at Christianity. That I am not a member of any Christian Church, is true; but I have never denied the truth of the Scriptures; and I have never spoken with intentional disrespect of religion in general, or of any denomination of Christians in particular. It is true that in early life I was inclined to believe in what I understand is called the 'Doctrine of Necessity' —that is, that the human mind is impelled to action, or held in rest by some power, over which the mind itself has no control; and I have sometimes (with one, two or three, but never publicly) tried to maintain this opinion in argument. The habit of arguing thus, however, I have entirely left off for more than five years. And I add here, I have always understood this same opinion to be held by several of the Christian denominations. The foregoing, is the whole truth, briefly stated, in relation to myself, upon this subject.

"I do not think I could myself, be brought to support a man for office, whom I knew to be an open enemy of, and scoffer at, religion. Leaving the high matter of eternal consequences between him and his Maker, I still do not think any man has the right thus to insult the feelings, and injure the morals, of the community in which he may live. If, then, I was guilty of such conduct, I should blame no man who should condemn me for it; but I do blame those, whoever they may be, who falsely put such a charge in circulation against me."

This was the only public statement Abraham Lincoln ever made about his faith.

He won the election by a decisive majority, polling 6340 votes against Cartwright's 4829. Of the $200 which his friends gave him for campaign expenses, he returned all but 75 cents. "I made the canvass on my own horse," he said, "my entertainment, being at the houses of friends, cost me nothing; and my only outlay was 75 cents for a barrel of cider, which some farmhands insisted I should treat to."

7. Congressman

The Thirtieth Congress did not convene till the last month in 1847, a year and a half after Lincoln's election. In the time between he rode the circuit, attended his law practice, and took cases as they came along. In one case he represented a slaveholder who sued for the return of an escaped slave family, having no qualms about prosecuting runaway slaves.

In October he leased his house for a year and set out with Mary and their two sons for Washington. They took rooms in Mrs. Spriggs' boarding house, but life in the capital was not to Mary's liking—within three months she and the children were on the way back to Springfield.

When Lincoln arrived in the capital the fighting in Mexico had already ceased. At the outbreak of the hostilities Henry Clay, the leader of the Whigs, had exclaimed: "This is no war of defense, but one of unnecessary and of offensive aggression." But soon the Whigs had realized that public opinion was backing the policies of President Polk; and that to try to pin the war guilt on the administration would not be a shrewd strategy.

In his addresses the President reiterated that it was Mexico who started the war, and not the United States. The Whigs questioned this. Lincoln submitted to the House an eight-point resolution, demanding from the President "whether the *spot* on which the blood of our citizens was shed . . . was or was not within a territory of Spain." Three weeks later he elaborated on his resolutions, asking that Polk, "a bewildered, confounded and miserably perplexed man," answer him "fully, fairly, candidly" whether "the soil was ours," and whether "the inhabitants had submitted themselves to the civil authority of Texas or of the United States."

Lincoln's constituents back home were bewildered; they had not voted for him to pursue such policies. His friends bombarded him with letters beseeching him to change his mind. The Democratic newspapers in the state assailed with mounting fury. The Peoria *Democratic Press* called him "a second Benedict Arnold"; the Springfield *Register* referred to him as "Spotty" Lincoln, an allusion to his spot resolution and the spotted fever sickness which was then rampant in Michigan. Wrote the *Register*: "This fever does not prevail to any alarming extent in Illinois. The only case we have heard of that is likely to prove fatal is that of 'Spotty' Lincoln of this state."

On other political issues his constituents had no quarrel with him. Lincoln was in support of the Wilmot Proviso, which declared that in all territories acquired from Mexico "neither slavery nor involuntary servitude shall ever exist," but he was against the agitation of the abolitionists, which, in his opinion, created only harm. Nevertheless his anti-war stand barred his re-nomination. He could not have a second term.

In the Whig convention of 1848 Lincoln supported General Zachary Taylor for the Presidency and campaigned for him in New England. Old Rough and Ready was elected and inaugurated, while Lincoln lingered in Washington. He tried his first and only case before the Supreme Court and he applied for a patent for an "Improved method of lifting vessels over shoals."

Returning to Springfield he fought a losing battle for a political plum—to become Commissioner in the General Land Office.

But later in the year, when the secretaryship and

governorship of the Oregon Territory were offered to him, he refused them.

He felt his political career was at an end; he thought that as a Congressman he had been a failure. He turned his back on politics and resumed his law practice.

8. *Family Matters*

People remember and talk and gossip Some of their stories are true, others are not.

Once neighbors saw Mary running her husband out of the house with a knife in her hand. It was Sunday morning and churchgoers were passing down the street, and they remembered that Lincoln forced her into the kitchen, shouting, "There, damn it, now stay in the house and don't disgrace us before the eyes of the world." Another time it was said he chased her around the block, screaming, "You make the house intolerable, damn you. Get out of it."

Did this really happen? Who can be sure of it? When they were apart—like the time Mary returned to Springfield to stay and Lincoln served his term in Congress—they sent letters to each other like people very much in love. Thus the lonesome husband wrote from Washington:

"In this troublesome world we are never quite satisfied. When you were here, I thought you hindered me some in attending to business; but now, having nothing but business—no variety—it has grown exceedingly tasteless to me. . . . I hate to stay in this old room by myself. . . ."

And Mary answered: "I feel wearied and tired enough to know, that this is *Saturday night*, our babies are asleep. . . . How much, I wish instead of writing, we were together this evening. I feel very sad away from you. . . ."

Lincoln was not an easy man to live with. Mary set

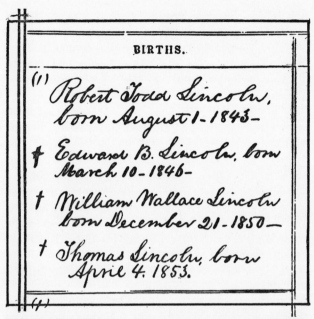

BIRTH RECORDS IN THE LINCOLN FAMILY BIBLE.

her mind on a neat household; her husband had sloppy habits. For the butter he used his old pocketknife. He liked to lie on the floor, reading, with the back of a chair for a pillow, coat and boots off, suspenders dangling from his trousers. In this untidy condition he one day answered a knock at the door, opening it to Mary's lady friends, while she raged over her husband's behavior.

On Sundays when Mary went to church, Lincoln was seen in shirt sleeves "hauling his babies in a little wagon up and down the pavement north and south on Eighth Street." And while he pushed the wagon he was reading a book, "so abstracted that the young one would fall out and squall, Lincoln moving on the while." Mary came out of church, saw the children on the street and gave her husband a tongue lashing.

After their domestic scenes Lincoln used to retreat to his office, sulking there silently, munching some cheese, crackers and bologna sausages, and not returning home till midnight, when Mary was already asleep.

Yet, their disagreements and irritations were overshadowed by a steady wave of affection and love. James Gourley, who lived next door for nineteen years, said that the Lincolns were good neighbors.

He recalled that Lincoln "kept his own horse, fed and curried it, fed and milked his own cow; he sawed his own wood generally when at home." He also remembered playing old-fashioned turn ball with his neighbor, and that Lincoln "hopped well; in three hops he would get 41 feet on a dead level."

Stories about the Lincoln children are legion, how their father adored them, how proud he was of them and how blind to their faults. There were four boys: Robert, Edward, William and Thomas. (Eddie died in 1850, the same year Willie was born.) They could do as they pleased. They raised havoc in the office, so that Herndon "wanted to wring their little necks," and he only kept silent because he knew how his partner "worshipped his children and *what* they worshipped; he loved what they loved and hated what they hated."

Lincoln had a forgiving soul. Yet when his father was dying, and his stepbrother suggested that he say farewell to the old man, he declined.

"Say to him that if we could meet now, it is doubtful whether it would not be more painful than pleasant; but that if it be his lot to go now, he will soon have a joyous meeting with many loved ones gone before; and where the rest of us through the help of God, hope ere long to join them."

He would not pretend affection, when he had none.

HIS EARLIEST PHOTOGRAPH. Taken by a Springfield daguerreotypist about 1846, seven years after Daguerre invented the photographic process. At the time of this sitting Lincoln was a representative to the Thirtieth Congress.

Lorant No. 2

FEBRUARY 28, 1857: Alexander Hesler, the well-known Chicago photographer who took this picture, recalled that as Lincoln's hair was "plastered down smooth over his forehead," he took the liberty to muss it up and arrange it.

MAY 7, 1858: On the day Lincoln's defense before the Beardstown Court cleared Duff Armstrong of the charge of murder, the photographer A. M. Byers persuaded the reluctant lawyer to visit his gallery and have his picture taken.

Lorant No. 5

JULY 11, 1858: At the outset of the senatorial campaign, a day after Lincoln spoke in Chicago in reply to Stephen A. Douglas. The full photograph shows Lincoln holding a Chicago *Press & Tribune*, whose editors supported him.

Lorant No. 6

AUGUST 26, 1858: A day before the Freeport debate, where Lincoln asked Douglas whether the people of a Territory could exclude slavery from its limits prior to formation of a State Constitution. Ambrotype by W. P. Pearson, Macomb.

OCT. I, 1858

OCT. 4, 1859

Lorant No. 14

FEBRUARY 27, 1860: On the day of the Cooper Union speech in New York, Lincoln went to Brady's Broadway studio. When Brady asked him to pull up his collar, Lincoln laughed: "I see you want to shorten my neck."

9. *Returning to Politics*

From 1849 till 1854 Lincoln was in political retirement experiencing "the invaluable discipline of defeat." And when the years were gone, he emerged from them stronger, "with the foundation of greatness firmly established and visible even to hostile eyes."

During these years he mastered a literary style, exact and much his own, based on the Bible and Shakespeare, but sparkling with stories of the land he knew so well. During these years he studied astronomy and mathematics, took in Euclid. These five years were years of growth.

The pattern of a country lawyer was a set one. Lincoln rode the Eighth Circuit through the unbroken prairie; he rode it in the sun and rode it in the rain, rode it in the wind and rode it in the snow. Hours and hours on horseback, time enough to think, time enough to contemplate.

Was he a good lawyer? His contemporaries believed so. "His knowledge of the law was acquired almost entirely by his own unaided study and by the practice of his profession," said one of his colleagues. Another mentioned that "he always tried a case fairly and honestly. He never intentionally misrepresented the testimony of a witness or the arguments of an opponent . . . He never misstated the law according to his own intelligent view of it."

Once he brought suit for a man to collect some money, and when the defendant proved that he had already paid the sum, Lincoln left the courtroom. The judge sent after him, but Lincoln told the messenger: "Tell the Judge that I can't come—my hands are dirty and I came over to clean them."

He sided with the needy. When a pension agent

claimed half her pension from the widow of a Revolutionary soldier, Lincoln sued the agent on behalf of the crippled old woman and, winning the case, he not only refused to accept a fee, but paid his client's hotel bill.

After the day's work, judge, lawyers and clients sat down to a dinner which at times lasted until the early hours of the morning. The subjects of their conversation ranged through the universe of thought and experience, with Lincoln always the central figure of the party. The three-hundred-pound hulk of Judge David Davis convulsed with laughter as he listened to his stories. "It was as a humorist that he towered above all men it was ever my lot to meet," recalled a man present.

But there were also days of darkness when he was silent, when he shunned company, when he walked the streets in lonely solitude, when "melancholy dropped from him." From boisterous happiness to morbid gloom the step was not far for him.

The circuit calendar over, he returned home and to his office. There he could be seen sitting with his legs stretched out upon another chair, reading or writing. If anyone came in, the visitor was greeted with a joke or anecdote. A student in the office remembered hearing him "relate the same story three times within as many

LINCOLN DEMANDS HIS FEE. "As the dutch Justice said, when he married folks 'Now, vere ish my hundred tollars.'"

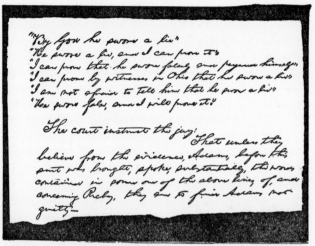

"By God he swore a lie"
"He swore a lie, and I can prove it"
"I can prove that he swore falsely and perjured himself"
"I can prove by witnesses in Ohio that he swore a lie"
"I am not afraid to tell him that he swore a lie"
"He swore false, and will prove it."

The court instruct the jury: That unless they believe from the evidence, Adams, before this suit was brought, spoke, substantially, the words contained in some one of the above lines of, and concerning Reely, they are to find Adams not guilty

LINCOLN INSTRUCTS THE JURY IN A SLANDER SUIT.

hours to persons who came in at different periods, and every time he laughed as heartily and enjoyed it as if it were a new story."

He was contented in his profession, earning a living and looking after the needs of his growing family. But when—at the beginning of 1854—Stephen A. Douglas, as chairman of the Senate Committee on Territories, introduced a bill to organize the territories of Kansas and Nebraska, Lincoln was roused "as he had never been before."

Why Douglas found it expedient to submit his bill and stir up a hornet's nest of political emotion remains an enigma. Most probably the building of the transcontinental railroad had something to do with it. If the Nebraska Territory was not organized speedily, the road might be built on a southern route. And Douglas, as Senator of Illinois, desired that the railroad should cross the northern states, with Chicago as its eastern terminus.

67

To secure this he needed Southern support, thus his proposals had to be made palatable to Southern political thinking. They incorporated the popular sovereignty principle, according to which the people of the new territories were to decide about the adoption or rejection of slavery within their borders.

The Douglas suggestion created a tremendous political storm. People in the North asked: Should a few settlers in the sparsely populated territories be allowed to decide on such vital issue without consulting the will of the whole country? And should the inhabitants of the territories have the right to vote on slavery even before their states are admitted to the Union? After three months of the most violent debates, Congress passed the Kansas-Nebraska Act, which in its final form repealed the restrictive feature of the Missouri Compromise. Whether below the 36° 30′ or above it, all states could now be legally opened to slavery.

The fury of the abolitionists, the anger of the antislavery advocates raged. Lincoln could no longer remain silent. Slowly and carefully—as was his nature—he made up his mind. In midsummer of 1854 he stumped his state for the re-election of his friend Richard Yates for Congress, arguing eloquently against Douglas's proposals and against the extension of slaveholding territory.

To clarify his position and explain his stand, Stephen A. Douglas came to Springfield to speak to his constituents. A day later, Lincoln replied to him at length; for three full hours he spoke in the torrid heat, coatless, collarless. On October 16, he repeated his arguments at Peoria, when his speech was reported fully.

In his Peoria address Lincoln declared that as the slavery issue had been settled by the Missouri Compromise of 1820 and the Compromise of 1850, there was no valid reason for repealing these measures. He admitted the South's constitutional right to hold slaves, but he denied that because of such right, slavery should be extended into the new territories. He held that it was wrong to let slavery into Kansas and Nebraska, "wrong in its prospective principle, allowing it to spread to every other part of the wide world, where men can be found inclined to take it." He said that he hated the zeal for the spread of slavery. "I hate it because of the monstrous injustice of slavery itself. I hate it because it deprives our republican example of its just influence in the world—enables the enemies of free institutions, with plausibility, to taunt us as hypocrites—causes the real friends of freedom to doubt our sincerity, and especially because it forces so many real good men amongst ourselves into an open war with the very fundamental principles of civil liberty—criticizing the Declaration of Independence, and insisting that there is no right principle of action but self-interest."

At the close of his passionate appeal Lincoln warned Douglas that it was not a matter of utter indifference whether a new country shall be slave or free. The great mass of mankind "consider slavery a great moral wrong; and their feeling against it is not evanescent, but eternal. It lies at the very foundation of their sense of justice; and it cannot be trifled with."

10. Joining the Republican Party

In the Illinois legislative election of 1854 the anti-Nebraska men carried the state. They were not a politically coherent group—Whigs, Democrats, and some of the new Republicans belonged to it, molded together and united only in the single purpose—their opposition to slavery. Yet, with a clear majority in the Legislature, they had the power to name one of their own men for the soon-to-be vacated senatorial seat (it must be remembered that senators were still elected by the Legislatures, and not by direct vote of the people).

Lincoln had his eye on the nomination; he would have liked to be junior senator, representing Illinois with Stephen A. Douglas in Congress. "During the anxious moments that intervened between the general election and the assembling of the Legislature, he slept, like Napoleon, with one eye open," noted Herndon. He wrote letters, lined up his supporters, and worked behind the scenes.

On the day of balloting it looked as if he might win. In the first trial he led with 44 votes against James Shield's 41 and Lyman Trumbull's 5. But when the Democrats switched from Shields to Governor Matteson, Lincoln released his supporters, asking them to vote for Lyman Trumbull, thus making him Senator. "I regret my defeat moderately," Lincoln wrote to a friend later, "but I am not nervous about it. I could have headed off every combination and been elected, had it not been for Matteson's double game—and his defeat now gives me more pleasure than my own gives me pain."

Keenly he watched the events in Kansas, where the principle of popular sovereignty was put to its first practical test. In the election for a territorial legislature, some 5000 armed men from Missouri swarmed over the border and stuffed the ballot boxes, assuring a pro-slavery legislature. Six months later the anti-slavery colonists repudiated the territorial legislature and asked for admission to the Union under a free-state constitution.

The Kansas struggle disrupted the country's political life. The parties split, slavery wing opposing anti-slavery wing. In the end the anti-slavery Whigs and Democrats banded together and formed the Republican party.

Lincoln, like other conservatives, was slow to join the new organization. Hesitant to take his part, he wrote to the abolitionist Owen Lovejoy on August 11, 1855: "Now even *you* are more anxious to prevent the extension of slavery than I; and yet the political atmosphere is such just now, that I fear to do anything, lest I do wrong."

But by the spring of 1856 his indecision waned. His name was among the signers calling an anti-Nebraska convention in Bloomington.

John Stuart, disturbed about his former law partner's political future, asked Herndon whether Lincoln really had signed "that Abolition call." And when Herndon admitted that it was he who had put Lincoln's name on the list, Stuart cried out: "Then you have ruined him." The disturbed Herndon wrote to Lincoln, then riding the circuit. Back came the answer. "All right; go ahead. Will meet you, radicals and all."

In this way he joined the Republican ranks; then the Bloomington convention marked the birth of the new party in Illinois. At that meeting Lincoln made a rousing speech. Herndon, who was present, noted: "I have heard or read all of Mr. Lincoln's great speeches, and I give it as my opinion that the Bloomington speech was the grand effort of his life. Heretofore he had simply argued the slavery question on grounds of policy—the statesman's ground—never reaching the question of the radical and the eternal right. Now he was newly baptized and freshly born; he had the fervor of a new convert; the smothered flame broke out; enthusiasm unusual to him blazed up; his eyes were aglow with an inspiration; he felt justice; his heart was alive to the right; his sympathies, remarkably deep for him, burst forth, and he stood before the throne of the eternal Right. His speech was full of fire and energy and force; it was logic; it was pathos; it was enthusiasm; it was justice, equity, truth, and right set ablaze by the divine fires of a soul maddened by the wrong; it was hard, heavy, knotty, gnarly, backed with wrath. I attempted for about fifteen minutes as was usual with me to take notes, but at the end of that time I threw pen and paper away and lived only in the inspiration of the hour. If Mr. Lincoln was six feet, four inches high usually, at Bloomington that day he was seven feet, and inspired at that."

Unfortunately, it was not only Billy Herndon who threw his pen and papers away. Thus nobody recorded the address; it became known as the celebrated "lost speech."

A fortnight after the Bloomington meeting the first Republican nominating convention assembled in Philadelphia, where in an informal ballot the delegates gave Lincoln 110 votes for the Vice-Presidency. Reading about it in his Springfield paper, he burst out: "I reckon that ain't me; there's another great man in Massachusetts named Lincoln, and I reckon it's him." Yet, in the final voting the convention chose not him but William L. Dayton as John C. Frémont's running mate.

11. *The Senatorial Contest*

In the presidential election of 1856 Lincoln spoke for the Republican ticket. But John C. Frémont lost; the new occupant of the White House was once more a Democrat: James Buchanan of Pennsylvania.

By the time of the new President's inauguration, disorders in Kansas had subsided. But two days later the Supreme Court's decision about the slave, Dred Scott, made passions flare up more strongly than ever before. In the court's opinion a Negro was not a citizen but property, and if a slave owner took his property into a territory where slavery did not exist, the law of that territory could not take it away from him. The decision inferred that Congress had no right to prohibit slavery anywhere in the United States; thus the Missouri Compromise, which forbade it over 36° 30′, was unconstitutional.

Senator Douglas quickly fell in line, submitting that if the Missouri Compromise was unconstitutional, its place must be taken by the popular sovereignty principle.

Lincoln challenged Douglas's contention in a speech at Springfield on June 26, 1857—his only public address of that year—arguing against the Dred Scott decision. Contrary to the Chief Justice's assumption that since the days of the Revolution the condition of the Negro race had improved, Lincoln contended that the colored man's "ultimate destiny has never appeared so hopeless as in the last three or four years." In the days of the Revolution, he said, "our Declaration of Independence was held sacred by all, and thought to include all; but now, to aid in making the bondage of the Negro universal and eternal, it is assailed, and sneered at, and construed, and looked at, and torn, till, if its framers could rise from their graves, they could not at all recognize it."

Lincoln ridiculed Douglas's "counterfeit logic" by which he claimed that the Republicans "want to vote, and eat, and sleep, and marry with Negroes." Why should anyone draw the conclusion that "because I do not want a black woman for a *slave* I must necessarily want her for a *wife*. I need not have her for either, I can just leave her alone. In some respects she certainly is not my equal; but in her natural right to eat the bread she earns with her own hands without asking leave of any one else, she is my equal, and the equal of all others."

In Lincoln's mind both Douglas and Chief Justice Taney were doing "obvious violence to the plain, unmistakable language of the Declaration." As he saw it, "authors of that notable instrument intended to include *all* men, but they did not intend to declare all men equal *in all respects*. They did not mean to say all were equal in color, size, intellect, moral developments, or social capacity. They defined with tolerable distinctness, in what respects they did consider all men created equal—equal in 'certain inalienable rights, among which are life, liberty, and the pursuit of happiness.' This they said, and this they meant."

Such reasoning won him new friends. His stand was clear, and appealing to the moderates. He pleaded for obedience to the laws, for upholding the Constitution. And as the laws of the country acknowledged slavery, so he was for protecting it, where it existed, but spoke against its further extension.

In the meanwhile the struggle in Kansas went on. The pro-slavery legislature of that state, meeting at Lecompton, proposed to submit an article of the constitution guaranteeing the right of property in slaves. Thus, whichever way the people voted, slavery would remain in that territory.

The North branded the Lecompton plan a fraud. And when President Buchanan, anxious to preserve his party's unity, recommended the admission of Kansas as a slave state, the outcry over his action shook the country. Senator Douglas condemned the Lecompton Constitution as a violation of the popular sovereignty idea, and he broke with the Administration. His term about to expire, Douglas would submit the issues to the electorate, confident that the voters of Illinois would endorse his policies.

74

Lincoln was ready to challenge Douglas, keen to win the Senatorship. But first he had to defeat the proposition of the Eastern politicians, who urged the Illinois Republicans to support the democratic Douglas in his fight against President Buchanan. Lincoln lived through anxious months.

With the coming of Spring, things looked up. On May 15, 1858, Lincoln wrote to a friend: "I think our prospects gradually, and steadily, grow better; though we are not yet clear out of the woods by a great deal. There is still some effort to make trouble out of 'Americanism.' If that were out of the way, for all the rest, I believe we should be out of the woods."

By June he was out of the woods. In that month the Republican State Convention of Illinois unanimously declared him to be its "first and only choice for the Senate," a slap against those who recommended Douglas.

Lincoln happily prepared an acceptance speech, but when he read it to his friends they were not impressed with it; they were critical of the passage which said: "A house divided against itself cannot stand. I believe this government cannot endure permanently half *slave* and half *free*. . . . It will become *all* one thing, or *all* the other." One of his friends thought it was "a damn fool utterance"; another, that it was "ahead of its time."

Lincoln would not change the criticized sentences and he remained always proud of that speech. Years later he said: "If I had to draw a pen across my record, and erase my whole life from sight, and I had one poor gift left as to what I should save from the wreck, I should choose that speech and leave it to the world unerased."

In his address he submitted: "Either the *opponents* of slavery will arrest the further spread of it, and place

75

it where the public mind shall rest in the belief that it is in the course of ultimate extinction; or its *advocates* will push it forward, till it shall become alike lawful in *all* the States, *old* as well as *new*, *North* as well as *South*."

And he predicted the coming of the day when the Supreme Court would declare that the Constitution did not allow a state to exclude slavery. "Welcome or unwelcome, such decision *is* probably coming, and will soon be upon us, unless the power of the present political dynasty shall be met and overthrown."

When Douglas learned that his opponent would be no one else but Lincoln, he burst out: "Of all the damned Whig rascals about Springfield, Abe Lincoln is the ablest and most honest . . . I shall have my hands full. He is the strong man of his party—full of wit, facts, dates—and the best stump speaker, with his droll ways and dry jokes, in the West."

The Little Giant made his first speech of the campaign in Chicago on July 9th. He tore into Lincoln's "house-divided" doctrine and pointed out that the nation had lived part slave and part free for eighty-two years; but now his opponent "goes for uniformity of our domestic institutions, for a war of sections until one or the other shall be subdued." Douglas repeated his political beliefs: "I go for the principle of the Kansas-Nebraska bill, the right of the people to decide for themselves."

The following night Lincoln answered his opponent's arguments from the balcony of the Tremont House. The Chicago *Press & Tribune* reported that his audience was only three-fourths as large as Douglas's, but "in point of enthusiasm, about four times as great." Lincoln took the issues one by one: Douglas's popular sovereignty principle, the Lecompton Constitution, the Dred Scott decision, and elaborated on them

Springfield, July 31. 1858.

Hon. S. A. Douglas.

Dear Sir

Your of yesterday, naming places, times, and terms, for joint discussion between us, was received this morning— Although, by the terms, as you propose, you take four openings and closes to my three, I accede, and thus close the arrangement— I direct this to you at Hillsboro; and shall try to have both your letter and this, appear in the Journal and Register of Monday, morning—

Your Obt. Servt.

A. Lincoln

ACCEPTING DOUGLAS'S TERMS FOR THE DEBATES.

with humor and hard facts. "Let us discard all this quibbling about this man and the other man," he concluded his address, "this race and that race and the other race being inferior, and therefore they must be placed in an inferior position—discarding our standards that we have left us. Let us discard all these things, and unite as one people throughout this land, until we shall once more stand up declaring that all men are created equal."

Thus the senatorial campaign had begun. Douglas set out in his private railroad car, his opponent hot on his trail. At times Lincoln travelled as a passenger on the train which drew Douglas's private car.

After they addressed meetings in Springfield, Lincoln challenged Douglas to a series of joint discussions.

Not long before the debates started, Lincoln met with a friend who was wondering whether he felt strong enough to stand up to Douglas. Lincoln replied: "You have seen two men about to fight? Well, one of them brags about what he means to do. He jumps high in the air, cracking his heels together, smites his fists, and wastes his breath trying to scare somebody. The other man says not a word. His arms are at his side, his fists doubled up, his head is drawn to the shoulder, and his teeth are set firm together. He is saving his mind for the fight, and as sure as it comes off he will win it, or die a-trying."

Their first debate was scheduled for Ottawa, on August 21st. By train, buggy, canal boat, horseback, and on foot the people came. Ten thousand voices cheered when the debaters mounted the platform; ten thousand men stood in the blazing sun for three full hours, listening to their arguments.

The meeting over, the enthusiastic Lincoln supporters carried their man off on their shoulders. In his subsequent addresses Douglas referred to this, saying: "Lincoln was so used up in the discussion that his knees trembled, and he had to be carried from the platform."

A week later they met at Freeport before a crowd of fifteen thousand. Lincoln asked Douglas whether, in view of the Dred Scott decision, the people of a territory could "in any lawful way, against the wish of any citizen of the United States, exclude slavery from its limits prior to the formation of a State Constitution?" Douglas replied that popular sovereignty was not incompatible with the Dred Scott decision. It was for the people to introduce or exclude slavery from the territories. If the majority of them were opposed to slavery, their elected representatives would "by unfriendly legislation, effectively prevent the introduction of it into their midst." This statement of Douglas became known as the Freeport doctrine.

The debates, colorful spectacles with brass bands

playing, military companies parading, cannons booming, glee clubs serenading the candidates, and fireworks lighting up the sky, continued at Janesboro, at Charleston, at Galesburg.

During Douglas's consistent attacks, Lincoln clarified his mind, revised and enlarged his thoughts. He no longer argued that the government "cannot endure permanently half slave and half free." He explained that he had no intention of making the house all free by interfering with slavery in the states where it already existed. All he wished was to reverse the trend.

In Quincy, the site of the sixth debate, Carl Schurz saw Lincoln for the first time and described him:

"On his head he wore a somewhat battered stovepipe hat. His neck emerged, long and sinewy, from a white collar turned down over a thin black necktie. His lank, ungainly body was clad in a rusty black dress coat with sleeves that should have been longer, but his arms appeared so long that the sleeves of a store coat could hardly be expected to cover them all the way down to the wrists. His black trousers, too, permitted a very full view of his large feet. On his left arm he carried a gray woolen shawl, which evidently served him for an overcoat in chilly weather. His left hand held a cotton umbrella of the bulging kind, and also a black satchel that bore the marks of long and hard usage."

The humorist David R. Locke, better known under his pen name of Petroleum V. Nasby, came for a visit and asked whether Lincoln thought he would win. No, he said, he did not expect to win, because of the gerrymandered districts, but he hoped to carry the state in the popular vote. "You can't overturn a pyramid, but you can undermine it; that's what I've been trying to do."

In the last debate—at Alton—Lincoln summed up

his beliefs: "The real issue in this controversy—the one pressing upon every mind—is the sentiment on the part of one class that looks upon the institution of slavery *as a wrong,* and of another class that *does not* look upon it as a wrong . . . They [the Republican party] look upon it as being a moral, social and political wrong; and while they contemplate it as such, they nevertheless have due regard for its actual existence among us, and the difficulties of getting rid of it in any satisfactory way and to all the constitutional obligations thrown about it . . . if there be a man amongst us who does not think that the institution of slavery is wrong in any one of the aspects of which I have spoken, he is misplaced and ought not to be with us."

The election results favored Douglas, though the Lincoln men polled four thousand more popular votes than the Douglas supporters. However, in the Legislature—which named the senator—Douglas had a clear majority—54 votes against Lincoln's 41.

When asked how he felt about his defeat, Lincoln came up with a story. He remembered that on election night as he walked home through the dark streets, "the path had been worn pig-backed and was slippery. My foot slipped from under me, knocking the other out of the way; but I recovered and said to myself, 'It's a slip and not a fall.' "

12. *Growing into a Candidate*

The debates made Lincoln's name known far outside the boundaries of his own state. In Illinois, newspaper writers began to mention him as a possible presidential candidate.

At first, he was hesitant to accept the call. To a newspaper editor eager to promote his candidacy he wrote:

"I must in candor say I do not think myself fit for the presidency." And when the editor insisted on alerting other Republican newspapermen in support of his nomination, Lincoln begged him: "I really think it best for our cause that no concerted effort, such as you suggest, should be made." But gradually he became reconciled to the idea. By the end of 1859 he no longer mentioned his unfitness for the Presidency; he behaved like a candidate.

In February 1860 he journeyed to New York, where he was to speak before the Young Men's Central Republican Union. The *Illinois State Register* in Springfield, the mouthpiece of the Democrats, commented sarcastically on the trip: "Subject not known, considered $200 and expenses. Object, presidential capital. Effect, disappointment."

The newspaper was far off the mark. More than 1500 people came to the Cooper Union to hear and cheer the lawyer from Illinois.

He began his address by agreeing with a statement of Senator Douglas that "our fathers, when they framed this government under which we live" understood the question of slavery. Delving into a lengthy examination of the background of the Constitution's thirty-nine signers and elaborating on their attitudes, he advised: "Speak as they spoke, and act as they acted upon it. This is all Republicans ask—all Republicans desire—in relation to slavery. As those fathers marked it, so let it be again marked, as an evil not to be extended, but to be tolerated and protected only because of and so far as its actual presence among us makes that toleration and protection a necessity. Let all the guaranties those fathers gave it, be, not grudgingly, but fully and fairly maintained. For this Republicans contend, and with this, so far as I know or believe, they will be content."

Lincoln denied that the North was sectional, denied that the Republicans were associated with the outrage of the abolitionist fanatic John Brown—who, the year before, had attempted to seize the Federal arsenal at Harper's Ferry—and he denied that the North desired to stir up insurrection among the slaves.

"What will satisfy the South?" he posed the question. "Simply this: we must not only let them alone, but we must somehow convince them that we do let them alone." Enlarging upon these thoughts he continued:

"Wrong as we think slavery is, we can yet afford to let it alone where it is, because that much is due to the necessity arising from its actual presence in the nation; but can we, while our votes will prevent it, allow it to spread into the national territories, and to overrun us here in the Free States? If our sense of duty forbids this, then let us stand by our duty, fearlessly and effectively."

Frequent applause interrupted the speaker. And when he ended, the cheering assemblage rose to its feet. "No man ever before made such an impression on his first appeal to a New York audience," reported the newspaperman Noah Brooks. "He's the greatest man since St. Paul."

After his Cooper Union lecture, Lincoln visited his eldest son, Robert, who was studying at Phillips Academy in New Hampshire's Exeter. He could stay with his son only for a short time; the demands for speeches were heavy. The visit over, he travelled through New England, spoke every day at a different town, speaking eleven times in as many days. The main theme of his speeches was slavery. In Hartford he said "One-sixth and a little more of the population of the United States are slaves looked upon as property, as nothing but property. The cash value of these slaves, at a moderate estimate, is $2,000,000,000. This amount of property value has a vast influence on the minds of its owners very naturally. The same amount of property would have an equal influence upon us if owned in the North." At New Haven he deviated from his subject to say a few words about the shoemakers' strike in Massachusetts. He ridiculed Douglas's contention that the strike arose from "this unfortunate sectional warfare," and then declared:

"I am glad to see that a system of labor prevails in New England under which laborers can strike when they want to, where they are not obliged to work under all circumstances, and are not tied down and obliged to labor whether you pay them or not! I like a system which lets a man quit when he wants to, and wish it might prevail everywhere." Cheering interrupted him. The audience liked what this lanky, strange-looking, midwestern lawyer had to say. "One of the reasons why I am opposed to slavery is just here. What is the true condition of the laborer? I take it that it is the best for all to leave each man free to acquire property as fast as he can. Some will get wealthy. I don't believe in a law to prevent a man from getting rich; it would do more harm than good. So while we do not propose any war upon capital, we do wish to allow the humblest man an equal chance to get rich with everybody else. When one starts poor, as most do in the race of life, free society is such that he knows he can better his condition; he knows that there is no fixed condition of labor, for his whole life."

The New England tour was a great success. On his return home, the Republican Club in Springfield welcomed him with the assurance that "No inconsiderable portion of your fellow citizens in various portions of the country have expressed their preference for you as the candidate of the Republican party for the next Presidency. . . ."

He was now an avowed contender. A steady stream of letters went to friends and politicians. "My name is new in the field," he wrote to a Republican lawyer in Columbus, Ohio, "and I suppose I am not the *first* choice of a very great many. Our policy, then, is to give no offence to others—leave them in a mood to come to us, if they shall be compelled to give up their first love." To Lyman Trumbull he confided that "the taste *is* in my mouth a little," and suggested: "You better write no letters which can possibly be distorted into opposition, or quasi opposition to me."

He had all advantages of an ideal candidate. He was against slavery, though he was neither a radical nor an abolitionist. His name was known, and yet not too well known; a politician of long standing, he had not been long enough in national politics to make too many enemies. And, as a son of Illinois, he would have the votes of a doubtful Republican state which were necessary for victory.

In the Illinois Republican State Convention old John Hanks, who had known him since childhood, marched down the aisle with two fence rails which he and Lincoln had supposedly split together. The delegates cheered, and Lincoln made a little speech. He was not sure, he said, whether he had made those rails some thirty years ago, but whether he made them or not, he had mauled better ones. After this impressive scene the convention resolved "That Abraham Lincoln is the choice of the Republican party of Illinois for the Presidency, and the delegates from his state are instructed to use all honorable means to secure his nomination by the Chicago Convention, and to vote as a unit for him."

13. *The Republican Convention*

The eyes of the country turned to Chicago, the big city with a hundred and ten thousand inhabitants, where the Republicans met to name their candidates.

Lincoln had remained in Springfield; candidates had no place at a nominating convention. But his managers were there in full force—Norman Judd and Stephen T. Logan, Richard Yates and Orville Browning, Joseph Medill of the Chicago *Press & Tribune* and Jesse Fell of the Bloomington *Pantagraph*. They were a dedicated lot—lawyers, editors, politicians—men who had travelled with him on the circuit, men who were his friends, who trusted and respected him. Led by the rich David Davis, the Judge of the Eighth Circuit, they were convinced that they could secure the nomination for Lincoln.

Their strategy was clear. The man to beat was William H. Seward, the acknowledged leader of the party and the most prominent contender for the nomination. Thus the task of the Lincoln managers was to rally all delegates who opposed Seward—those who were against him because of his radical stand on slavery, those who were uneasy about choosing a man who re-

THE WIGWAM AT CHICAGO, where the Republicans met in May 1860 in a nominating convention and chose Lincoln.

ferred to the controversy as an "irresistible conflict" and who exclaimed that "there is a higher law than the Constitution." They had to convince the delegates that Lincoln "excited no hates anywhere" and "has made no records to be defended or explained," and who was the man who could unite behind him all Republicans.

The managers argued that to win the election the Republicans needed the votes of Pennsylvania, Indiana, Illinois and New Jersey, therefore they must select a candidate who was able to carry these doubtful states. At the outset they had only the votes of Illinois, but they worked on the other delegations, offering bargains, making promises, trading patronage for votes. When Lincoln heard about this in Springfield he wired them: "I authorize no bargains and will be bound by none." One of his managers cursed. "Damn Lincoln!" and they kept on bargaining, cajoling, courting, flattering, promising, regardless of their candidate's feelings.

Indiana was won over by the promise to make Caleb B. Smith, the chairman of the Hoosier delegation, Secretary of the Interior and William P. Dole Commissioner of Indiana Affairs.

John A. Andrew, the chairman of the Massachusetts delegation, urged his colleagues from New Jersey, Pennsylvania, Indiana and Illinois to settle behind one candidate and not to scatter the votes among three. "Now it is impossible to have all these three candidates," said Andrew, "and unless you delegates from the four doubtful states can agree upon some one candidate, who you think can carry these states, we from New England will vote for our choice, William H. Seward of New York; but if you will unite upon some one candidate and present his name, we will give him enough votes to place him in nomination."

With the votes of Illinois and Indiana secured, the

THE REPUBLICAN HOPEFULS, as presented by *Harper's Weekly* shortly before the Chicago convention. In the center: William H. Seward, the favorite contender for the nomination. On the left: Edward Bates, a conservative lawyer from Missouri; William Pennington of New Jersey; Salmon P. Chase of Ohio; John C. Frémont, the Republicans' choice in 1856; Abraham Lincoln. On the right: Nathaniel P. Banks of Massachusetts; Judge John McLean of Ohio, Simon Cameron of Pennsylvania; John Bell, who later became the nominee of the Constitutional Unionist party; Cassius M. Clay, the ardent old abolitionist from Kentucky.

Lincoln men went after the 56 votes of Pennsylvania. The night before the balloting, Judge David Davis emerged from the rooms of the Pennsylvanians. "Damned if we haven't got them!" he cried out. A friend asked him: "How did you get them?" And Davis answered: "By paying their price"—the price being the Secretaryship of the Treasury, which was to go to Simon Cameron, the Pennsylvania political boss. "Good heavens!" groaned the friend, "give Cameron the Treasury Department? What will be left?"

"Oh, what's the difference?" retorted Davis. "We are after a bigger thing than that; we want the Presidency, and the Treasury is not a great stake to pay for it."

That same night two other of Lincoln's managers hit on the idea of printing counterfeit tickets to the convention hall and distributing them among their supporters. Thus, when morning dawned, the Wigwam was packed with men who, admitted on the duplicates, were ready to shout and hurrah Abraham Lincoln into nomination.

The Seward contingent, confident of victory, paraded through the streets of Chicago and when they reached the hall all the seats were already taken. It was of little use to wave their tickets in fury; the convention hall was filled to the beams; they had to remain outside.

Amid intense excitement, the balloting for the candidates began. The first trial brought no surprises. Maine gave ten votes to Seward and six to Lincoln; Vermont was for its favorite son, Senator Collamer; Massachusetts cast 21 for Seward and four for Lincoln; Rhode Island's majority went to Judge McLean, Connecticut's to Bates. New York with its 70 votes was behind Seward; New Jersey behind its "favorite son," Dayton; Pennsylvania's majority also voted for the state's "favorite son," Simon Cameron; Maryland and Delaware were for Bates; Virginia gave eight votes to Seward and fourteen to Lincoln; Kentucky's vote was divided among five candidates: Seward, Lincoln, Chase, McLean, Sumner; Ohio's majority went to Chase. Indiana was solidly for Lincoln, Missouri for Bates; Michigan, Wisconsin and the majority of Texas were for Seward. Iowa was divided. California and Minnesota

Lorant No. 16

MAY 8, 1860: A week before the Chicago nominating convention. Photograph by E. A. Barnwell, Decatur, Illinois.

Lorant No. 18

MAY 20, 1860: A day after Abraham Lincoln received formal notice that the Republican party had named him as its candidate for the Presidency. The ceremony was held in the parlor of his Springfield home. Photograph by W. Church

JUNE 3, 1860: "The dressed up candidate." As the Republicans needed a good vote-getting picture of their man, Alexander Hesler journeyed to Springfield and posed Lincoln for a series of portraits, later used in the campaign.

Lorant No. 28

SUMMER OF 1860: Photographers, painters and sculptor descended on the Republican candidate after his nomination They all wanted his likeness. This expressive portrait of Lin coln was made by an unknown man, probably in August

SUMMER OF 1860: Another picture taken in Springfield while Lincoln kept his council and remained silent about his policies, so that his words should not be misconstrued. The photograph might be the work of William Seavy.

SUMMER OF 1860: A not long ago discovered profile, found in the papers of biographer Ida Minerva Tarbell.

AUGUST 13, 1860: The silent candidate. An ambrotype taken by Preston Butler in Springfield, Illinois.

**SUMMER
OF 1860**
L i n c o l n
only full-fi
ure phot
graph befo
he becan
President.
was probab
made for t
s c u l p t c
L e o n a r
Wells Vol
who used it
a model for
a portrait bu

supported Seward; Oregon was behind Bates. The territories of Kansas and Nebraska and the District of Columbia gave 10 out of a total of 14 to Seward.

The result: Seward led with 173½ votes, Lincoln was next with 102, followed by Cameron with 50½, Chase with 49 and Bates with 48, and there were scattered votes for the lesser contenders.

On the second ballot Lincoln's strength increased by 79 votes. He had now only 3½ votes less than Seward; 181 votes to the favorite's 184½.

The hall was in an uproar. "Call the roll, call the roll," shouted the delegates with impatience.

To win the nomination, 233 votes were necessary. In the third ballot Lincoln gained four votes in Massachusetts, one in Rhode Island, four in Pennsylvania, nine in Maryland. When he was only 1½ votes short of success, Joseph Medill, one of Lincoln's managers, whispered to David Cartter, chairman of the Ohio delegates: "If you can throw the Ohio delegation to Lincoln, Chase can have anything he wants." We will never know whether or not these words influenced Cartter, but he got on his feet in an instant and stammered in the deadly quiet hall:

"I-I a-a-rise, Mr. Chairman, to a-a-nnounce the c-ch-change of f-four votes from Mr. Chase to Mr. Lincoln."

Pandemonium broke loose. The Lincoln supporters danced down the aisles, threw their hats in the air, sang and whistled. One of them rushed to the telegraph office and wired to Springfield: "We did it. Glory to God."

Lincoln received the news in the *Journal* office. And after it came, and after his supporters had shaken his hand and slapped him on his back and called him Mr. President, he bade them goodbye: "Well, gentlemen, there is a little short woman at our house who is probably more interested in this dispatch than I am; and if you will excuse me, I will take it up and let her see it." And he walked through the deserted streets to bring Mary the news.

14. *The Election*

In his temporary office at the Springfield State House, the Republican candidate received a steady stream of visitors. Artists set up their equipment to paint him, sculptors to mold his head, photographers to take his likeness.

Lincoln resolved not to "write or speak anything upon doctrinal points." He would not issue statements on policy, as "those who will not read or heed what I have already publicly said, would not read, or heed, a repetition of it."

When asked to reassure the "honestly alarmed" men over the unrest in the South, he said that in his opinion there were no such men: "It is the trick by which the South breaks down every Northern man. If I yielded

LINCOLN STORMS THE WHITE HOUSE. The other contenders, John Bell, Stephen A. Douglas and John C. Breckinridge (helped by President Buchanan), try also to get in.

LINCOLN WEIGHS THE OYSTERS. At left: the "softshell" Democratic candidate, Stephen A. Douglas; at right: John C. Breckinridge, the "hardshell" pro-slavery contender.

to their entreaties I would go to Washington without the support of the men who now support me. I would be as powerless as a block of buckeye wood. The honest men . . . will find in our platform everything I could say now, or which they would ask me to say."

They certainly could. As Horace Greeley, one of its drafters, believed that "An Anti-Slavery man *per se* cannot be elected; but a tariff, River and Harbor, Pacific Railroad, Free Homestead man may succeed," the Republican platform promised all good things to all good people. The tariff plank attracted the Eastern protectionists, the homestead plank appealed to those who sought land; river and harbor improvements found supporters in the Northwest; the plank against immigration restrictions was championed by the German and other foreign groups.

The outlook for a Republican victory looked bright. The Democrats entered the campaign with two sets of candidates. Their Northern wing chose Stephen A.

CAMPAIGN CARTOONS FROM 1860

ABRAHAM WINNING THE BALL GAME. A Currier and
Ives cartoon shows the four candidates: Lincoln, Douglas,
Breckinridge and Bell, in an early game of baseball.

LINCOLN ATOP A WOODPILE, sheltering a negro beneath
him. Horace Greeley argues with "Young America" that
"we have no connection with the Abolition Party," but the
voter says: "I can see the nigger peeping through the rails."

THE RAIL CANDIDATE. Lincoln, carried by a Negro and Horace Greeley on a rail marked the Republican platform, comments wryly that "it's the hardest stick I ever straddled."

Douglas, while their Southern faction named John C. Breckinridge, the representative of the slaveholding interests. There was also the Bell-Everett ticket, put to the fore by a group of former Whigs and Know Nothings. These conservatives rallied the Constitutional Union party under the motto: "The Constitution of the country, the Union of the States, and the enforcement of the laws." With three candidates splitting the votes, the Republicans were certain to win. In the election they carried all the Northern states but New Jersey, which was divided. In the South eleven out of the fifteen slave states upheld Breckenridge, three states voted for Bell, and only one—Missouri—was for Douglas. Of the popular vote, Lincoln received 1,866,-452, Douglas 1,376,957, Breckenridge 849,781, and Bell 588,879. Thus Abraham Lincoln was to be the next President of the United States.

15. *President-Elect*

From the election till the inauguration—from November till March—was a long way. The country was in a turmoil and in the South the secession sentiment grew; the President-elect was implored to say some placating words. But Lincoln remained silent. To the editor of the *Missouri Republican* he wrote: "I could say nothing which I have not already said, and which is in print and accessible to the public. Please pardon me for suggesting that if the papers, like yours, which heretofore have persistently garbled, and misrepresented what I have said, will now fully and fairly place it before their readers, there can be no further misunderstanding." In his confidential communications he reassured his Southern friends of his peaceful intentions. To Alexander Stephens, who later became the Vice-President of the Confederacy, he sent a note "for your own eye only," in which he reduced the differences between North and South to the single sentence: "You think slavery is *right* and ought to be extended; while we think it is *wrong* and ought to be restricted. That I suppose is the rub."

But the time for peaceful arguments had gone. In his annual message—in December, 1860—President Buchanan said that "while a State could not lawfully secede, neither could the Federal Government coerce it." Thus he suggested the calling of a Constitutional Convention which was to guarantee slavery in the states and territories and assuring the recovery of fugitive slaves. The South would not hear of it. On December 20 South Carolina broke away from the Union, followed by Mississippi, Florida, Alabama, Georgia and Louisiana, and a little later by Texas. Federal forts and arsenals were taken over; the Stars and Stripes were hauled down.

Men of good will looked desperately for a compromise. Senator Crittenden proposed a number of amendments to the Constitution which would guarantee slavery where it already existed, continue the slave trade, indemnify the owners of fugitive slaves, and extend the Missouri Compromise line to the Pacific.

Lincoln would have gone along with many of Senator Crittenden's proposals, but he would not submit to the extension of slavery, would not agree to its spread into the territories.

"Let there be no compromise on the question of *extending* slavery," he wrote to Senator Lyman Trumbull. "If there be, all our labor is lost, and, ere long, must be done again. The dangerous ground—that into which some of our friends have a hankering to run—is Pop. Sov. Have none of it. Stand firm. The tug has to come, & better now, than any time hereafter."

Lincoln was still hopeful that a final break between North and South could be avoided. He felt that the secessionists could be restrained by their loyal brethren. Eight of the fifteen slave states were still in the Union. If they could be kept from breaking away, he hoped that the seceded states might reconsider their actions.

It was a trying time, a time of anxiety, a time taxing all of Lincoln's patience. His room was crowded steadily with politicians and office-seekers. Every mail brought basketfuls of letters with warnings and advice. Outside his home petitioners were lying in wait for him, using the pavement for their sleeping quarters. His law office was beleaguered. Everywhere he went he was followed by a crowd.

An eleven-year-old girl—Grace Bedell—wrote him that he would look a great deal better with a beard "for your face is so thin." Lincoln answered that as he had never worn any whiskers, "do you not think people would call it a piece of silly affection if I were to begin it now?" But hardly a month had gone by when he was seen with stubble sprouting from his chin. The

United States had never had a bearded President. For a new era Lincoln was producing a new profile.

The immediate problem was the formation of the Cabinet. After protracted consideration, talks and negotiations, the list emerged. William H. Seward of New York became Secretary of State; Salmon P. Chase of Ohio, Secretary of the Treasury; Gideon Welles, a former Democrat editor from Connecticut, Secretary of the Navy. The border states were represented by Edward Bates, an anti-slavery lawyer who became Attorney General, and Montgomery Blair, a member of the influential political family, who was named Postmaster General. To pay off the convention bargains, Caleb B. Smith of Indiana was made Secretary of the Interior, and Simon Cameron, a political boss from Pennsylvania, Secretary of War.

In his spare moments Lincoln worked on his inaugural. And as the time drew near, he locked himself

FRIENDS AND OFFICE-SEEKERS came in droves to see the President-elect in his office at the State House.

Springfield, Ills Oct 19. 1860

Miss Grace Bedell

My dear little Miss.

Your very agreeable letter of the 15th is received—

I regret the necessity of saying I have no daughter— I have three sons— one seventeen, one nine, and one seven, years of age— They, with their mother, constitute my whole family.

As to the whiskers, having never worn any, do you not think people would call it a piece of silly affection if I were to begin it now?

Your very sincere well-wisher
A. Lincoln

LINCOLN'S REPLY to the eleven-year-old school girl who suggested that he should grow a beard. "As to the whiskers," he wrote her, "having never worn any, do you not think people would call it a piece of silly affection if I were to begin it now?" But a few weeks later he had a beard.

up in a back room over his brother-in-law's store and with four references at his elbow—the Constitution, Andrew Jackson's proclamation against nullification, Webster's reply to Hayne, and Henry Clay's speech on his 1850 compromise proposal—he composed his address. And when he had finished it, a compositor at the *Journal* office set it up and pulled a few proofs of it.

Sunday, February 10, 1861, was his last day in Springfield. He walked over to his law office to clear his desk and to say goodbye to his law partner Herndon. After the unfinished business was disposed of, he threw himself down on the old office sofa, lying there in meditation.

"Billy, how long have we been together?" he asked.

"Over sixteen years."

"We've never had a cross word during all that time, have we?"

"No indeed, we have not."

Lincoln was in a cheerful mood, reminiscing of the past. Then he gathered a bundle of books and papers and started to go. He told Herndon not to remove the signboard at the foot of the staircase.

"Let it hang there undisturbed," he said in a low voice. "Give our clients to understand that the election of a President makes no change in the firm of Lincoln and Herndon. If I live I'm coming back some time, and then we'll go right on practicing law as if nothing had ever happened."

Early next morning the railway station was crowded with men and women who had come to bid him fare-

SELLING THE FURNITURE. Before he left for Washington, Lincoln rented his house and sold some furniture. Six chairs brought $12, a spring mattress $26, and a whatnot $10.

HIS FAREWELL TEXT. After the train left Springfield, the journalist Henry Villard asked the President-elect for his speech. Lincoln began to write it out, but as the train rocked, John Nicolay took over and continued the writing.

well. As his train was about to pull out, Lincoln appeared on the back platform of his car and spoke:

"My friends, no one, not in my situation, can appreciate my feeling of sadness at the parting. To this place, and the kindness of these people, I owe everything. Here I have lived a quarter of a century, and have passed from a young to an old man. Here my children have been born, and one is buried. I now leave, not knowing when, or whether ever, I may return, with a task before me greater than that which rested upon Washington. Without the assistance of that Divine Being, who ever attended him, I cannot succeed. With that assistance I cannot fail. Trusting in Him, who can go with me, and remain with you, and be everywhere for good, let us confidently hope that all will yet be well. To His care commending you, as I hope in your prayers you will commend me, I bid you an affectionate farewell."

Then the train pulled out, leaving friends and neighbors, home and early life behind.

16. *First Inaugural*

The journey to Washington took twelve days. Everywhere his train stopped, he spoke. At every station he exhorted the people to do their utmost for the preservation of the Union. "If the Union of these states, and the liberties of this people, shall be lost," he said at Indianapolis, "it is but little to any one man of fifty-two years of age, but a great deal to the thirty millions of people who inhabit these United States, and to their posterity in all coming time. It is your business to rise up and preserve the Union and liberty, for yourselves, and not for me. I desire they shall be constitutionally preserved."

Arriving at Philadelphia Allan Pinkerton, the head of a private detective agency, warned the President-elect of an impending plot against his life and pleaded with him to avoid the city of Baltimore, where assassins were lying in wait. Lincoln would not heed the warning. But when another report came, this time from Washington, he acquiesced in the change of his traveling schedule. He would slip away from Harrisburg accompanied by his friend Ward Hill Lamon and

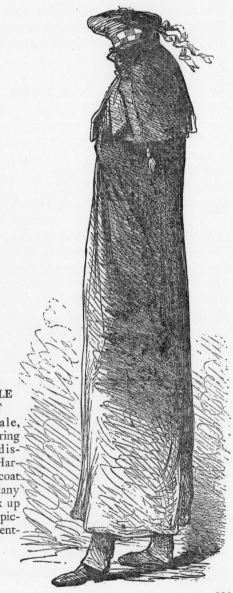

AN IRRESPONSIBLE JOURNALIST invented the tale, that Lincoln, fearing assassination, disguised himself at Harrisburg in a plaid coat and Scotch cap. Many caricaturists took up the rumor and pictured the President-elect in disguise.

no one else. And he would put on a soft hat and an old overcoat to escape recognition. An irresponsible reporter enlarged on this incident; thus the newspapers pictured Lincoln as a coward who must disguise himself in fear of assassination.

The special carriage reached Baltimore in the early hours of the morning and was drawn through the streets by a horse from one station to the other. Reaching the capital, the excitable little Pinkerton wired in code: "PLUMS (meaning Lincoln) ARRIVED HERE WITH NUTS (Lamon's code name) THIS MORNING ALL RIGHT."

Soon after his arrival in Washington, Lincoln met with members of the Peace Conference. He told the delegates, who tried to restore unity to a nation already divided: "My course is as plain as a turnpike road. I am in no doubt which way to go. Suppose now we all stop discussing and try the experiment of obedience to the Constitution and the laws. Don't you think it would work?"

The weather on inauguration day was like the mood of the nation—clear skies alternated with dark clouds. The rumor spread that Lincoln would never take the oath, that assassins would kill him long before. The military commanders of the capital were alert. Riflemen on the roofs of the houses along Pennsylvania Avenue watched the windows of the buildings with orders "to fire upon them in case any attempt should be made to fire from those windows on the presidential carriage."

At noon President James Buchanan called on the President-elect at his hotel, and together they rode down Pennsylvania Avenue. After witnessing the swearing-in of his running-mate, Hannibal Hamlin, Lincoln was escorted to the portico, where his old friend Edward Dickinson Baker made the introduction.

ON THE WAY TO THE INAUGURATION. Accompanied by President Buchanan, Lincoln rides along Pennsylvania Ave.

Lincoln searched for a place to put his shiny new hat; tradition has it that Stephen A. Douglas stepped forward and held it for him. Then taking from his pocket the sheaf of printed galleys—the set of proofs of his address which the compositor in Springfield had pulled for him secretly and which now bore many written revisions—he adjusted his spectacles and began to read his address. "Apprehension seems to exist among the people of the Southern States, that by the accession of a Republican Administration, their property, and their peace, and personal security, are to be endangered," he said. But in his opinion, there had never been any reasonable cause for such apprehension. "I have no purpose, directly or indirectly, to interfere with the institution of slavery in the states where it exists. I believe I have no lawful right to do so, and I have no inclination to do so."

To allay Southern fears he gave his solemn promise that he would hold strictly to the words of the fugitive slave law, which "is as plainly written in the Constitution as any other of its provisions." He reminded his listeners that the Constitution had come into being to form a more perfect Union. "But if destruction of the Union, by one, or by part only, of the States, be lawfully possible, the Union is *less* perfect than before, which contradicts the Constitution, and therefore is absurd."

He declared that the Union was unbroken and that the laws of the Union would be faithfully executed in all the States. "Doing this I deem to be only a simple

THE INAUGURATION: FROM A MAGAZINE OF 1861.

The Chief Magistrate derives all his authority from the people, and they have conferred none upon him to fix terms for the separation of the States. The people themselves can do this *also* if they choose; but the executive, as such, has nothing to do with it. His duty is to administer the present government, as it came to his hands, and to transmit it, unimpaired by him, to his successor.

Why should there not be a patient confidence in the ultimate justice of the people? Is there any better or equal hope, in the world? In our present differences, is either party without faith *of being* in the right? If the Almighty Ruler of nations, with his eternal truth and justice, be on ~~either your~~ *on your side of the North, or on yours of the South,* that truth and that justice, will surely prevail, by the judgment of this great tribunal, the American people.

By the frame of the government under which we live, this same people have wisely given their public servants but little power for mischief; and have, with equal wisdom, provided for the return of that little to their own hands at very short intervals. While the people *retain their virtue, and vigilence, no administration* ~~retain~~ by any extreme of wickedness or folly, can very seriously injure the government in the short space of four years.

☞ My countrymen, one and all, *think calmly and* ~~well~~ upon this whole subject. Nothing valuable can be lost by taking time. ~~Such... ~~ If there be an object to *hurry* any of you, in hot haste, to a step which you would never take *deliberately,* that object will be frustrated by taking time; but no good object can be frustrated by it. Such of you as are now dissatisfied, still have the old Constitution unimpaired, and, on the sensitive point, the laws of your own framing under it; while the new administration will have no immediate power, if it would, to change either. If it were admitted that you who are dissatisfied, hold the right side in the dispute, there still is no single good reason for precipitate action. Intelligence, patriotism, Christianity, and a firm reliance on Him, who has never yet forsaken this favored land, are still competent to adjust, in the best way, all our present difficulty.

7746   In *your* hands, my dissatisfied fellow countrymen, and not in *mine,* is the momentous issue of civil war. The government will not assail *you,* ~~unless you~~ You can have no conflict, without being yourselves the aggressors. *You* have no oath registered in Heaven to destroy the government, while *I* shall have the most solemn one to "preserve, protect and defend" it. ~~I... ~~ *"☞ I am loth to close. We are not enemies, but friends. We must not be enemies. Though passion may have strained, it must not break our bonds of affection. The mystic chords of memory, stretching from every battle-field, and patriot grave, to every living heart and hearthstone, all over this broad land, will yet swell the chorus of the Union, when again touched, as surely they will be, by the better angels of our nature.*

THE INAUGURAL ADDRESS. Since put in type in Springfield, Lincoln had revised many times and enlarged it. Secretary of State Seward suggested the concluding sentences.

duty on my part; and I shall perform it so far as practicable, unless my rightful masters, the American people, shall withhold the requisite means, or, in some authoritative manner, direct the contrary."

Then he argued: "In doing this there needs to be no bloodshed or violence; and there shall be none, unless it be forced upon the national authority. The power confided to me will be used to hold, occupy, and possess the property and places belonging to the government, and to collect the duties and imposts; but beyond what may be necessary for these objects, there will be no invasion—no using of force against, or among the people anywhere."

Turning to those "who really love the Union," he emphasized that "the central idea of secession is the essence of anarchy." Substantially, the dispute is that "one section of our country believes slavery is *right*, and ought to be extended, while the other believes it is *wrong*, and ought not to be extended."

But, in his belief: "Physically speaking, we cannot separate. We cannot remove our respective sections from each other, nor build an impassable wall between them. . . . This country, with its institutions, belong to the people who inhabit it. Whenever they shall grow weary of the existing government, they can exercise their *constitutional* right of amending it, or their revolutionary right to dismember, or overthrow it." He asked the country to think on the subject calmly and well. "Nothing valuable can be lost by taking time."

He turned his words plainly to the South: "In *your* hands, my dissatisfied fellow-countrymen, and not in *mine* is the momentous issue of civil war. The government will not assail *you*. You can have no conflict, without being yourselves the aggressors. *You* have no oath registered in Heaven to destroy the government, while *I* shall have the most solemn one to 'preserve, protect and defend' it."

Originally this was the end of his address. But when William Seward proposed a final conciliatory paragraph, Lincoln reworked Seward's cold sentences into a prose of Biblical beauty:

"I am loth to close. We are not enemies, but friends. We must not be enemies. Though passion may have

THE OATH WAS GIVEN BY CHIEF JUSTICE TANEY.

strained, it must not break our bonds of affection. The mystic chords of memory, stretching from every battle-field, and patriot grave, to every living heart and hearthstone, all over this broad land, will yet swell the chorus of the Union, when again touched, as surely they will be, by the better angels of our nature."

Then he took the oath, and from thousands of throats came the cheer for the sixteenth President of the United States.

Part Two

1. *What He Looked Like*

His law partner, Billy Herndon, who observed Lincoln during his twenty-four years' stay in Springfield, described him this way:

"Mr. Lincoln was six feet four inches high, and when he left the city of his home for Washington was fifty-one years old, having good health and no gray hairs, or but few, on his head. He was thin, wiry, sinewy, rawboned; thin through the breast to the back, and narrow across the shoulders; standing he leaned forward—was what may be called stoop-shouldered, inclining to be consumptive by build. His usual weight was one hundred and eighty pounds. His organization—rather his structure and functions—worked slowly. His blood had to run a long distance from his heart to the extremities of his frame, and his nerve force had to travel through dry ground a long distance before his muscles were obedient to his will. His structure was loose and leathery; his body was shrunk and shriveled; he had dark skin, dark hair, and looked woe-struck. The whole man, body and mind, worked slowly, as if it needed oiling. Physically he was a very powerful man, lifting with ease four hundred, and in one case six hundred pounds. His mind was like his body, and worked slowly but strongly. Hence there was very little bodily or mental wear and tear in him. This peculiarity in his construction gave him great advantages over other men in public life. . . .

"When he walked he moved cautiously but firmly; his long arms and giant hands swung down by his side.

He walked with even tread, the inner sides of his feet being parallel. He put the whole foot flat down on the ground at once, not landing on the heel; he likewise lifted his foot all at once, not rising from the toe, and hence he had no spring to his walk. His walk was undulatory—catching and pocketing tire, weariness, and pain, all up and down his person, and thus preventing them from locating. The first impression of a stranger, or a man who did not observe closely, was that his walk implied shrewdness and cunning—that he was a tricky man; but, in reality, it was the walk of caution and firmness. In sitting down on a common chair he was no taller than ordinary men. His legs and arms were abnormally, unnaturally long, and in undue proportion to the remainder of his body. It was only when he stood up that he loomed above other men.

"Mr. Lincoln's head was long, and tall from the base of the brain and from the eyebrows. His head ran backwards, his forehead rising as it ran back at a low angle, like Clay's and unlike Webster's, which was almost perpendicular. The size of his hat measured at the hatter's block was seven and one-eighth, his head being, from ear to ear, six and one-half inches, and from the front to the back of the brain eight inches. Thus measured it was not below medium size. His forehead was narrow but high; his hair was dark, almost black, and lay floating where his fingers or the winds left it, piled up at random. His cheek-bones were high, sharp, and prominent; his jaws were long and upcurved; his nose was large, long, blunt, and a little awry towards the right eye, his chin was sharp and upcurved; his eyebrows cropped out like a huge rock on the brow of a hill; his long sallow face was wrinkled and dry, with a hair here and there on the surface; his cheeks were leathery, his ears were large, and ran out almost at right angles from his head, caused partly by heavy hats and partly by nature; his lower lip was thick, hanging, and undercurved, while his chin reached for the lip upcurved; his neck was neat and firm, his head being well balanced on it; there was the lone mole on the right cheek, and Adam's apple on his throat.

"Thus stood, walked, acted and looked Abraham Lincoln. He was not a pretty man by any means, nor was he an ugly one; he was a homely man, careless of his looks, plain-looking and plain acting. He had no pomp, display, or dignity, so-called. He appeared simple in his carriage and bearing. He was a sad looking man; his melancholy dripped from him as he walked."

John G. Nicolay, Lincoln's secretary, who also pondered over the President's features, added these observations to Herndon's pen portrait:

"The question of looks depended in Lincoln's case very much upon his mood," wrote Nicolay. "The large framework of his features was greatly modified by the emotions which controlled them. The most delicate touch of the painter often wholly changes the expression of a portrait; his inability to find that one needed master touch causes the ever-recurring wreck of an artist's fondest hopes. In a countenance of strong lines and rugged masses like Lincoln's the lift of an eyebrow, the curve of a lip, the flash of an eye, the movements of prominent muscles created a much wider facial play than in rounded immobile countenances. Lincoln's features were the despair of every artist who undertook his portrait. . . . Graphic art was powerless before a face that moved through a thousand delicate gradations of line and contour, light and shade, sparkle of the eye and curve of the lip, in the long gamut of expression from grave to gay, and back again from the rollicking jollity of laughter to that serious, faraway look that with prophetic intuitions beheld the awful panorama of war, and heard the cry of oppression and suffering.

There are many pictures of Lincoln; there is no portrait of him."

The poet Walt Whitman agreed with Nicolay:

"None of the artists have caught of the deep, though subtle and indirect expression of this man's face. They have only caught the surface. There is something else there. One of the great portrait painters of two or three centuries ago is needed."

And Gustave Koerner summed up these feelings in the simple sentence:

"Something about the man, the face, is unfathomable."

2. Fort Sumter

A day after his inauguration a report of grave portent reached President Lincoln's desk. It came from Major Robert Anderson, commander of Fort Sumter, the last remaining fort in Federal hands in the harbor of Charleston. Anderson sent word that his provisions were running low and that if he could not be supplied within six weeks he would have to abandon the fort.

Thus, at the outset of his administration a momentous decision—a decision on which hung the peace of the country—faced the new President. In his inaugural address he had promised to "hold, occupy, and possess" places and property belonging to the Federal government. But if he were to supply Fort Sumter, the seven seceded states might resist it with arms. And not to supply the garrison would prove that the new administration had not the courage of its convictions.

Fort Sumter grew to be a symbol. For the North the holding of the fort meant the preservation of Federal authority; for the South the flying of the Stars and Stripes within the territory of a seceded State, humiliation and an insult.

Lincoln knew that by taking aggressive action at Fort Sumter, the lower South would be drawn into a war, and once hostilities began, the loyal slave states, too, might break away. Therefore, he played for time, asking advice of the Cabinet and of high military and naval authorities. His hesitation seemed like weakness. Newspaper writers accused him of drifting without a course, without a firm policy.

The Secretary of State offered some "thoughts for the President's consideration," in which he advised that "whatever policy we adopt, there must be an energetic prosecution of it. For this purpose it must be somebody's business to pursue and direct it incessantly. Either the President must do it himself, and be all the while active in it, or devolve it on some members of his Cabinet." The President reminded Seward that if a thing must be done, "I must do it." He would not relinquish his responsibilities.

The situation in Virginia kept him worried. The Virginia State Convention, though loyal to the Union, would not adjourn so long as the Federal government maintained an intransigent attitude towards her sister State, South Carolina. Lincoln hoped that by settling the Sumter controversy peacefully, Virginia could be kept within the Union. "If you will guarantee me the State of Virginia I shall remove the troops," he said to a Unionist member of the Convention. "A State for a fort is not bad business," he was heard to say. But no promise was forthcoming.

Despite his firm inaugural declaration, he thought earnestly about giving up Sumter. To make this palatable to Northern public opinion and to uphold Northern prestige, he intended to reinforce Fort Pickens off Pensacola Harbor in Florida. Thus, in the first week of April he ordered two expeditions to be ready, one for Florida, the other to South Carolina. If the Pickens ex-

Lorant No. 35

NOVEMBER 25, 1860: Lincoln's first portrait with a beard. Newspapermen joked about his changing face: "Old Abe is puttin' on (h)airs!" Never before, they commented, had the United States had a bearded President. Lincoln was the first.

121

JANUARY, 1861: The beard had grown longer, but it still does not "belong" to his face. He looks strange with it. Dr. Baringer says that Lincoln's beard signified the coming of the new era. For a new life he had created a new profile.

122

Lorant No. 37

FEBRUARY 9, 1861: The last photograph made in Spring-field before his departure to Washington. He had already roped his trunks and labeled them "The White House." In two days he would leave, never to return again.

BEFORE OCTOBER 3, 1861: Lincoln inscribed this photograph on October 3, 1861, to the mother of his Springfield friends Joshua and James Speed, "from whose pious hand I accepted the present of an Oxford Bible twenty years ago."

1862: A photograph taken by Mathew B. Brady in Washington. The furrows on the President's face had grown deeper; the anxieties of the first war year had left their indelible marks. It is a tragic portrait, one of Brady's best.

Lorant No. 54

1863: THE YEAR OF THE EMANCIPATION PROCLAMAT

★

Lorant N

NOVEMBER 1863:
SHORTLY BEFORE THE GETTYSBURG ADDR

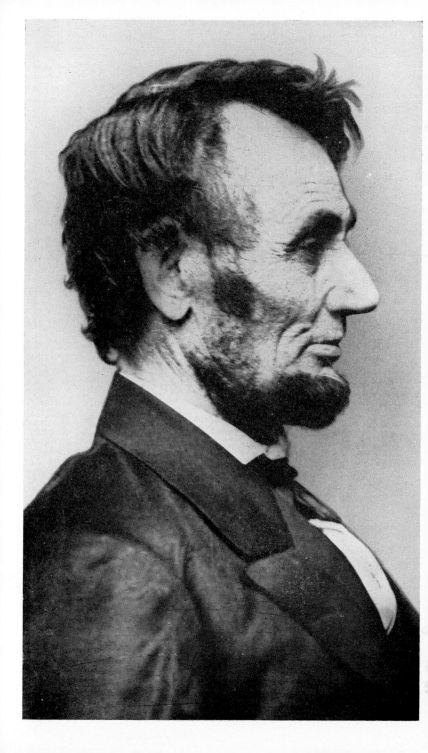

FEBRUARY 9, 1864: This portrait and the profile opposite were taken by Mathew B. Brady in his Washington studio in one of the most elaborate sittings. Lincoln took Tad with him, and Brady photographed them together. (see p. 164)

APRIL 26, 1864: This portrait—unknown for more than eight decades—was discovered by the author of this volume. It was taken by Brady for the artist Carpenter, who used it as a model for his Emancipation Proclamation painting.

1864: One of the few photographs of Lincoln during his Presidency which were not taken by Brady or Gardner, but by Thomas Walker, an employee of the Treasury Department and an outstanding amateur photographer.

1864

1865

HIS

LAST

PHOTO-

GRAPHS

Lorant Nos. 84, 85 and 86

APRIL 10, 1865:
After his return from
City Point, Lincoln
visited Alexander
Gardner's studio to
have a picture taken.
It was his last visit to
a photographer; four
days later, on Good
Friday, the assassin's
bullet felled him.

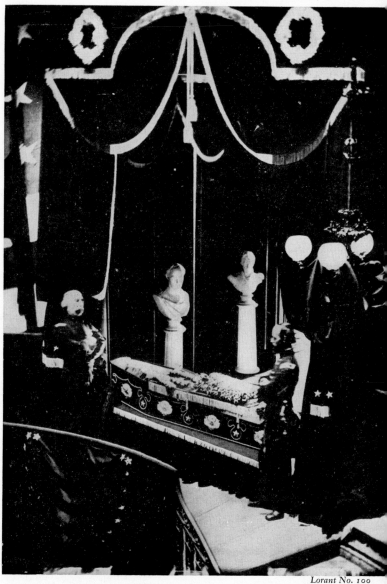

Lorant No. 100

APRIL 24, 1865: Abraham Lincoln lying in state in New York's City Hall. A recently discovered print, taken by Gurney & Son, which had been confiscated by Secretary of War Stanton and remained lost for eighty-seven years.

pedition was successful, Sumter would be surrendered. But when the Federal naval commander at Pensacola would not allow the landing of Union troops for the fort, Lincoln had no alternative but to reinforce Sumter.

The Governor of South Carolina was notified of the Federal government's intention to provision Fort Sumter, and advised that neither additional troops nor arms would be sent to the fort. The Governor communicated the message to the Confederate government in Alabama, which replied that the Confederacy would no longer suffer the presence of Federal troops within the territory of a seceded state and demanded the immediate surrender of Fort Sumter. And when this was not forthcoming, at the dawn of April 12, 1861, the batteries of Charleston opened fire against the fort. The fratricidal struggle which Lincoln prayed to avoid became a reality.

The outbreak of the war erased Lincoln's indecision. No longer hesitant, no longer wavering, he issued a proclamation declaring that as the laws of the country were opposed in the seven seceded states "by combinations too powerful to be repressed by the course of judicial proceeding," he was compelled to call on the states of the Union for 75,000 troops of their militia "to suppress the said combinations." Force was to be met by force; the challenge of the South against the Federal authority would not be tolerated.

A few weeks later, in his first message to Congress, the President explained: "The assault upon the reduction of Fort Sumter was in no sense a matter of self defense on the part of the assailants. They well know that the garrison in the fort could by no possibility commit aggression upon them. They knew—they were expressly notified—that the giving of bread to the few brave and hungry men of the garrison was all which would on that occasion be attempted, unless themselves, by resist-

THE BOMBARDMENT OF FORT SUMTER, as depicted by a contemporary *Harper's Weekly* artist. During the early hours of April 12, 1861, the inhabitants of Charleston climbed to their housetops to watch the bursting shells.

ing so much, should provoke more." The blame could not be put on the North; it was the South who was to bear the guilt.

"They knew that this Government desired to keep the garrison in the Fort, not to assail them, but merely to maintain visible possession, and thus to preserve the Union from actual, and immediate dissolution—trusting, as herein before stated, to time, discussion, and the ballot-box, for final adjustment; and they assailed, and reduced the Fort, for precisely the reverse object— to drive out the visible authority of the Federal Union and thus force it to immediate dissolution."

The firing on the flag at Fort Sumter, so Lincoln rea-

138

soned, forced upon the country the distinct issue: immediate dissolution, or blood. "And this issue embraces more than the fate of these United States. It presents to the whole family of man, the question, whether a constitutional republic, or a democracy—a government of the people, by the same people—can, or cannot, maintain its territorial integrity, against its own domestic foes. It presents the question, whether discontented individuals, too few in numbers to control administration, according to organic law, in any case, can always, upon the pretences, or arbitrarily, without any pretence, break up their Government, and thus practically put an end to free government upon the earth. It forces us to ask: 'Is there, in all republics, this inherent, and fatal weakness?' 'Must a government, of necessity, be too *strong* for the liberties of its own people, or too *weak* to maintain its own existence?' "

Thus, "viewing the issue, no choice was left but to call out the war power of the Government; and so to resist force, employed for its destruction, by force, for its preservation."

"We must settle this question now," he said somberly, "whether in a free government the minority have the right to break up the government whenever they choose. If we fail it will go far to prove the incapability of the people to govern themselves."

3. *War*

The war began, as all wars do, with flagwaving and exultation and song. As always, both sides had supreme confidence. As always, both sides boasted about their strength, both sides disdained the opponent's weakness. And as always, both sides were convinced of the rightness and justness of their cause.

North and South were unequal in strength. The

population of the twenty-two loyal states numbered about twenty million; the population of the eleven seceded states (after Lincoln's call for troops, Virginia, North Carolina, Arkansas and Tennessee joined the Confederacy) was about six million, not counting the slaves. Northern industry, resources and manpower were vastly superior to those of the South, but in fighting spirit and military leadership the South had the advantage. Southerners made good soldiers; they knew how to handle a rifle and how to ride a horse. They came from the land, they were hunters and farmers—not artisans, factory workers, city dwellers, like most of the soldiers from the North.

To Southerners the purpose of the fight seemed clear; they believed that every state had the right to secede, and once such a decision was reached, the Federal government had no authority to interfere. For the South, the North was the aggressor; the South only entered the war to keep its freedom and independence from Northern domination, to hold onto its way of life.

The purpose of the North could not be made so easy to understand. Ideas are always more difficult to explain. The North went into the struggle, not for the eradication of slavery, but for the principle that in a free government the minority has not the right to break up the government at will.

The outbreak of war multiplied the President's worries; it increased his duties. He had to raise an army. The North had only 16,000 men under arms, of which number no more than 3,000 could be detached for service in the East. He worked relentlessly to unify the various shades of opinion in the North and to keep the dubiously loyal border states—Kentucky, Missouri and Delaware—within the Union. It was a gigantic task, requiring all his patience, energy and skill.

To organize the country for war, keep disgruntled politicians in line and watch friends and foes with ever vigilant eyes, demanded all his waking hours. Yet most of his time was taken up by office seekers. Each day, the grounds, halls, stairways of the Executive Mansion teemed with applicants. One after the other went notes to members of the Cabinet, one recommending a Marshal for Vermont, another an agent for the Ponca tribe in Dakota, still another the appointment of the Consul General of Canada—a steady stream of memoranda was penned by the President, giving judgeships, postmasterships, consulships to the faithful. When a friend saw Lincoln's depressed face, he asked whether the President had bad news from the army. "No," came the reply, "it isn't the army, it's the post office at Brownsville, Missouri."

After the bombardment of Fort Sumter, troops were ordered to the undefended Capital. Washington was in an uneasy mood; the Confederates had 15,000 men at nearby Alexandria. Maryland secessionists had torn up the railroad tracks and severed telegraphic communications; the Capital became isolated. For days there was no sign of the Massachusetts, Rhode Island and New York troops, who were on the way. Watching for them with a telescope, Lincoln burst out in anguish: "Why don't they come! Why don't they come!"

At Baltimore, secessionist sympathizers attacked the Sixth Massachusetts Regiment as it marched through the city. Four dead and many wounded remained on the street. When the regiment reached Washington and the wounded men came to pay their respects to the President, Lincoln told them with bitterness: "I begin to believe that there is no North. The Seventh Regiment is a myth. Rhode Island is another. You are the only real thing."

To a delegation of Baltimore citizens who came to

demand that no more Federal troops should be marched
through their city, Lincoln replied in short temper:

"You, gentlemen, come here to me and ask for peace
on any terms, and yet have no word of condemnation
for those who are making war on us. You express great
horror of bloodshed, and yet would not lay a straw
in the way of those who are organizing in Virginia
and elsewhere to capture this city. The rebels attack
Fort Sumter, and your citizens attack troops sent to
the defense of the Government, and the lives and property in Washington, and yet you would have me break
my oath and surrender the Government without a
blow. There is no Washington in that—no Jackson in
that—no manhood nor honor in that. I have no desire to
invade the South; but I must have troops to defend the
Capital. Geographically it lies surrounded by the soil
of Maryland; and mathematically the necessity exists
that they should come over her territory. Our men are
not moles, and can't dig under the earth; they are not

ON THE WAY TO THE CAPITAL, the Sixth Massachusetts
Regiment was attacked by Rebel sympathizers while passing through Baltimore. In the riot four soldiers were killed.

142

"TURN BACK! TURN BACK! We are whipped," cried the Union men as they fled from the battlefield. In the first great encounter of the Civil War, on July 21, 1861, the Federals under General Irvin McDowell were defeated at Bull Run.

birds, and can't fly through the air. There is no way but to march across, and that they must do."

By early summer about 35,000 Federal troops under the command of General Irwin McDowell were in training. Newspapers and politicians urged impatiently, "On to Richmond!" The free states, eager for action, clamored for an offensive, believing that at the first blow the rebellion would collapse.

Pressed from all sides, and realizing that the clash of arms would strengthen the unity of the North, Lincoln ordered General Irwin McDowell to move against the Confederates. On a hot Sunday, July 21, 1861, the Federal army crossed the little creek of Bull Run and attacked the Confederates at Manassas, about fifteen miles southwest of Washington. At first the advantage was with the North, but when General Johnston's army joined up with the main Southern force under Beauregard, the Confederates counterattacked, and the Union troops fled in panic.

That night the President remained in the Cabinet room, listening to the tales of eyewitnesses who had gone to the battlefield in their carriages to witness the victory of the Union arms: and were treated with the spectacle of defeat.

Reports on the following day showed that the result was not as disastrous as first believed. The War Department announced: "Our loss is much less than was first represented, and the troops have reached the forts in much better condition than we expected." The fortifications on the south bank of the Potomac were in good order and were well manned. And it became evident that the Confederates could not follow up their victory. "Our army was more disorganized by victory," said General Johnston later, "than that of the United States by defeat." And Stonewall Jackson declared that if he could have had 10,000 fresh troops, "I would be in Washington to-day." But there were no 10,000 fresh troops—neither for the Union nor the Confederacy.

For the North the defeat at Bull Run was a blessing in disguise. The burden of internal discord waned; the people grew more united in their war effort.

In the South the jubilation over Bull Run led to false hopes. Soldiers left their units and started for home; politicians believed that the victory would be followed by European recognition of the Confederacy and help in breaking the blockade.

Lincoln saw that he needed a stronger man than McDowell to head the army. Thus, the day after Bull Run he sent for General George Brinton McClellan.

The new commander was thirty-five years old, self-confident and vigorous. He had graduated from West Point, served in the Mexican War, and been a military observer in the Crimean War. Resigning his commission, he was appointed chief engineer and vice-president of the Illinois Central Railroad, then became head of the Mississippi and Ohio Railroad.

After the bombardment of Fort Sumter he led the Ohio Volunteers; then was commissioned Major General of the army, in command of the Department of Ohio. In western Virginia his successful campaign cleared the territory of Confederate forces.

McClellan, a student of military tactics, was an able organizer. Small of stature, brash, and self-assured of his own abilities, his soldiers endearingly called him "Little Mac" or "Little Napoleon." But his virtues were more than evenly balanced by his shortcomings. He was overcautious, he hesitated to move into action unless he believed everything was in his favor. Forever he waited for a certainty. In his notes one finds sentences like: "So soon as I feel that my army is well organized and well disciplined, and strong enough, I will advance." Or: "I feel sure of to-morrow." For him there was always the hope of a "to-morrow." In steady anxiety over the superior manpower of the Confederates, he constantly pleaded for more troops and more equipment.

But whatever his faults, he proved highly effective in organizing the army into an efficient fighting force. The recruits were trained under rigid discipline, the defenses of Washington were strengthened, preparations for a forthcoming offensive made. By the end of the year 170,000 well-equipped men were under arms.

The North, understanding that a new army needed training, waited patiently, but when fall came and there was still the report "All quiet along the Potomac," the restlessness mounted, and the President was pressed to send the General into battle.

McClellan, so he told his political friends, favored

145

an offensive if only his hands were not tied. He complained that the General in Chief, Winfield Scott, was set on a defensive strategy. "Gen. Scott is the obstacle," he wrote: "He will not comprehend the danger. I have to fight my way against him. Tomorrow the matter will probably be decided by giving me absolute control independently of him. I suppose it will result in enmity on his part against me; but I have no choice. The people call on me to save the country. I must save it, and cannot respect anything that is in my way."

McClellan's mind worked in a curious way. He looked upon those who were against his ideas not only as evil men, but as traitors. He despised General Scott and all other military and political leaders. "It is sickening in the extreme, and makes me feel heavy at heart, when I see the weakness and unfitness of the poor beings who control the destinies of this great country," he cried out.

Seventy-five-year-old General Winfield Scott, infirm with dropsy and vertigo, tired of the brash young General's behavior, sent Lincoln his resignation the last day of October. The President reluctantly accepted it, and on the following day named McClellan as General in Chief of the army.

A short time after the General's appointment, the President, accompanied by Secretary of State Seward and John Hay, went to McClellan's house to discuss military matters. As McClellan was absent, Lincoln decided to wait. An hour later the General arrived and, "without paying any particular attention to the porter, who told him the President was waiting to see him, went upstairs, passing the door of the room where the President and Secretary of State were seated. They waited about half an hour, and once more sent a servant to tell the General they were there, and the answer coolly came that the General had gone to bed."

Lincoln left the house quietly, telling his enraged Secretary that "it was better at this time not to be making points of etiquette and personal dignity."

The President kept on urging the General to attack before the wintry roads would prohibit operations. McClellan would not be hurried—probably from the first he intended to wait for spring—and before he was ready to take his army against Richmond, bad weather set in, and the move had to be postponed. The great Army of the Potomac went into winter quarters; and the year of 1861 came to an end.

4. *Dark Months*

1862 opened under dark clouds. In the East the Army of the Potomac idled in camp, in the West the leading commanders could not co-ordinate their operations.

The abolitionists were still fuming with anger because a few weeks earlier the President had revoked General Frémont's proclamation which gave freedom to the slaves in the territory under his command. Senator Charles Sumner derided Lincoln as a dictator, "but how vain to have the power of a God and not use it godlike." He was assailed not only by the anti-slavery men; censure came even from his erstwhile political supporters, and this hurt him deeply. To the reproach of Orville Browning, good friend since Vandalia days, Lincoln replied in a long letter, patiently explaining his motives.

"Genl. Frémont's proclamation," he wrote, "as to confiscation of property, and the liberation of slaves, is *purely political*, and not within the range of *military* law, or necessity. If a commanding general finds a necessity to seize the farm of a private owner, for a pasture, and encampment, or a fortification, he has the right to do so, and to so hold it, as long as the necessity lasts; and this is within military law, because within military necessity. But to say the farm shall no longer belong to the owner, or his heirs forever; and this as well when the farm is not needed for military purposes as when it is, is purely political, without the savor of military law about it. And the same is true of slaves. If the General needs them, he can seize them, and use them; but when the need is past, it is not for him to fix their permanent future condition. That must be settled according to laws made by law-makers, and not by military proclamations. The proclamation in the point in question, is simply 'dictatorship.' It assumes that the General may do *anything* he pleases—confiscate the lands and free the slaves of *loyal* people, as well as of disloyal ones. And going the whole figure I have no doubt would be more popular with some thoughtless people, than what has been done! But I cannot assume it on my responsibility. You speak of it as being the only means of *saving* the government. On the contrary it is itself the surrender of the government. Can it be pretended that it is any longer the Government of the U.S.—any government of Constitution and laws—wherein a General, or a President, may make permanent rules of property by proclamation?"

Lincoln pointed out that the political results of Frémont's declaration, if not revoked, would have proven disastrous for the Northern cause. It would have created ill feeling in the border states and would have put the loyalty of Kentucky to a severe test. And if Kentucky were lost to the Union, it "is nearly the same as to lose the whole game. Kentucky gone, we can not hold Missouri, nor, as I think, Maryland. These all against us, and the job on our hands is too large

VICTORIES FOR THE NORTH. The blows on Jefferson Davis's face are marked Fort Donelson, Fort Henry, and Nashville; the cut on Lincoln's cheek is labelled: Bull Run.

for us. We would as well consent to separation at once, including the surrender of this capitol."

The list of the President's troubles was a long one. There were the difficulties with England because two Confederate commissioners had been forcibly removed from a British ship. And even after the commissioners were set free, the ill feeling lingered on.

There were the difficulties with the radicals in his own party. Congress formed a joint Committee on the Conduct of War, which harassed him and encroached on his prerogatives. Generals were called to testify. Those whose beliefs coincided with those of the committee were treated with courtesy, others were pilloried, their reputations smeared.

There were irregularities inside the War Department. The buying of rotten blankets, rotten boots and rotten knapsacks for the troops from men who politically supported the administration caused discontent. Simon Cameron, the Secretary of War, was a weak and slovenly man, his eyes closed to graft and corruption. As soon as he could, Lincoln relieved him of the post and appointed in his stead Edwin M. Stanton.

There were the usual difficulties with General McClellan. And they became unusual when the General fell seriously ill, kept to his bed, and brought the affairs of his army to a standstill.

"What shall I do?" cried out Lincoln in desperation. "The people are impatient; Chase has no money, and tells me he can raise no more; the General of the army has typhoid fever. The bottom is out of the tub. What shall I do?"

He was seriously thinking of taking over the direction of the military operations. But when McClellan recovered and came to Washington, Lincoln allowed him to go on with his plans. To prod Little Mac into action, Lincoln issued the curious "General War Order No. 1," directing that on February 22, 1862, an all-out movement of the land and naval forces of the United States was to commence against the insurgent forces.

To the political and military difficulties was added private sorrow. In February twelve-year-old Willie Lincoln died, leaving his father prostrate with grief. He moaned: "My poor boy, he was too good for this earth." He refused food and paced the floor for hours in deep thought. He proposed that Thursday, the day of Willie's death, should be set aside as a day of national mourning for the families who had lost sons in the war.

The alarmed Mary begged the Reverend Dr. Francis Vinton to see her husband. The minister came and told Lincoln that indulgence in his grief, though natural, was sinful and unworthy of one who believed in the Christian religion. "Your son is *alive*, in Paradise. Do you remember that passage in the Gospels: 'God is not the God of the *dead*, but of the living, for *all* live unto him'? Lincoln repeated through his tears, "Alive? alive?" and the clergyman answered: "See not your son among the dead; he is not there; he lives today in Paradise."

They were desperate months, those early months of 1862. The Union, weary of the war, was sorely in need of a military victory.

5. *Commander-in-Chief*

Spring came, Spring of 1862, and the Army of the Potomac was still in camp.

McClellan made his plans with great caution. He would take the army by boats to Fortress Monroe, then move it up the region between the York and James rivers, known as the Peninsula, against the Confederate capital. Lincoln was not taken with the strategy, yet he consented to its execution when eight of McClellan's division commanders voted in its favor. But he stipulated that sufficient troops be left for the defense of the Capital.

At last, on April 1, the first Union troops landed at Fortress Monroe. But even as the army moved into position, McClellan—who in the meantime had been restricted to the command of the Army of the Potomac—complained that he had not enough men. He resented bitterly that the President had retained General McDowell's corps for the defense of Washington, and bewailed that he was not properly sustained. Lincoln replied that the General's dispatches "do pain me very much," and that his allegations about not being "properly sustained" were without foundation. He told the General: "I think it is the precise time for you to strike a blow. By delay the enemy will relatively gain upon you—that is, he will gain faster, by *fortification* and *reinforcements* than you can by reinforcements alone."

McClellan was not the man to listen to such advice. It took more than a month before Yorktown fell. On May 6, a day after the Confederates evacuated the city, Lincoln came to Fortress Monroe to encourage and prod his slow-moving commander. He promised the dispatch of more troops, though later, when Stonewall Jackson moved up the Shenandoah Valley and threatened the safety of Washington, McDowell's army was sent into the Valley and not to the Peninsula. Lincoln had no desire for "swapping queens," to give up Washington for the occupation of Richmond.

The President kept in close touch with his commanders. He wired them, often several times during a single day. Let us take a characteristic day, May 24, 1862, when he made the decision not to let McDowell's troops go to the Peninsula. At 4 P.M. he telegraphed McClellan: "In consequence of Gen. Banks' critical position I have been compelled to suspend Gen. McDowell's movement to join you. The enemy are making a desperate push upon Harper's Ferry, and we are trying to throw Frémont's force & part of McDowell's in their rear."

An hour later—at 5 P.M.—he directed General McDowell "to put twenty thousand men (20,000) in motion at once for the Shenandoah moving on the line of or in advance of the line of the Manassas Gap R Road." Another wire ordered General Frémont "to move against Jackson on Harrisonberg and operate against the enemy in such way as to relieve Banks. This movement must be made immediately." At 7:15 P.M. a second telegram was sent to Frémont: "Much—perhaps all—depends upon the celerity with which you can execute it [the order]. Put the utmost speed into it. Do not lose a minute."

Colonel Miles was asked: "Could you not send scouts from Winchester, who would tell whether enemy are north of Banks, moving on Winchester? What is the latest you have?" General Saxton was questioned: "Please inform us, if possible, what has become of the force which pursued Banks yesterday."

Before the sun set, Lincoln related to McClellan the events in the other theaters of operation and suggested: "If in conjunction with McDowell's movement against Anderson you could send a force from your right to cut off the enemy's supplies from Richmond, preserve the Rail Road bridges across the two forks of the Pamunkey and intercept the enemy's retreat you will secure a line of Rail Road for supplies in addition to the one you now have. Can you not do this almost as well as not, while you are building the Chickahominy bridges?"

Reading these telegrams, there could be no mistake; Lincoln was not commander-in-chief in name only, he had an active part in all military planning.

Two days later, on May 26, when McClellan was within sight of Richmond, the President wired him: "I think the time is near when you must either attack Richmond or give up the job and come to the defense of Washington." By then the Army of the Potomac had been nearly two months in the Peninsula, advancing only sixty miles.

The last day in May, General Johnston, seeing that McClellan's army was on both sides of the swollen Chickahominy, attacked the Federals near Fair Oaks and Seven Pines. The battle lasted for two days, with losses for both sides, but without decisive result.

It was at Fair Oaks that General Johnston, the Confederate commander, was severely wounded and had to relinquish his command. General Robert E. Lee became the new commander of the Southern army. Lee, who

Washington City, D.C.
June 3 1862

Maj. Gen. McClellan

With their continuous rain, I am very anxious about the Chickahominy so close in your rear, and crossing your line of communication— Please look well to it.

A. Lincoln

THE WORRIED LINCOLN kept in constant touch with the commanders in the field. The above dispatch is one of many sent to General McClellan during the Peninsular Campaign.

knew McClellan well, and of whom it was said that he could read McClellan like an open book, realized that Little Mac was waiting for reinforcements. To attack him before the arrival of these reinforcements became his aim.

On June 26 the Confederates launched their assault. For a whole week—the Battle of the Seven Days— the two armies fought valiantly. The Federals lost 16,-000 men, the Confederates 20,000.

McClellan extricated himself from the Confederates' attacks and retreated sixteen miles to Harrison's Landing, where he entrenched his position. For his failure he had blamed the President and his constant meddling with military strategy. "If I save this army now," he wrote in a dispatch to the Secretary of War, "I tell you plainly that I owe no thanks to you or to any other persons in Washington. You have done your best to sacrifice this army."

Little Mac was fuming in anger.

6. *In Search of a General*

The North needed fresh blood to replenish the ranks. Asking the Governors for recruits, Lincoln assured them that the contest would be maintained until successful, "or till I die, or am conquered, or my term expires, or Congress or the Country forsake me."

On the first day of July 1862, when a call for 300,000 volunteers was issued, the President told General McClellan: "It is impossible to re-inforce you for your present emergency. If we had a million of men we could not get them to you in time. We have not the men to send. If you are not strong enough to face the enemy you must find a place of security, and wait, rest and repair. Maintain your ground if you can; but save the Army at all events, even if you fall back to Fortress Monroe. We still have strength enough in the country, and will bring it out."

At the outset of the Presidency, Lincoln's knowledge of military matters was perfunctory. But as the war went on, he mastered strategy and logistics, his mind grasping the problems quickly. Yet he felt the need of a military adviser, a man to whom he could turn and whose counsel he could ask. Thus, when he returned from Harrison's Landing, where he had visited McClellan on July 8, he called General Henry W. Halleck to the East and appointed him "to command the whole land forces of the United States, as General-in-Chief."

Halleck was young, forty-seven, though from his pictures one would think him twenty years older. He had brusque manners, seemed insincere and aloof, but he had the reputation of being shrewd and smart. "Old Brains" translated books from the French on military theory and wrote original works on military problems.

Had he possessed a different character, Halleck's appointment to the supreme command could have been successful. But, as Professor T. Harry Williams, in his masterly *Lincoln and His Generals*, explains: "He was supreme commander in name but rarely in fact. He provided Lincoln with military advice, which was sometimes accepted, but he exercised little actual control over military operations. His tenure of command was an experiment in unified direction of the armies that did not work out well because he disliked responsibility and did not want to direct. He delighted to counsel but he hated to decide. Nevertheless, the experiment was necessary, and for Lincoln it was educational. The government was groping toward a modern command system, and Lincoln learned much from his experience with Halleck."

The immediate military problem before Lincoln was whether McClellan's army should be left in the Peninsula, be reinforced for another attack against Richmond, or ordered back and combined with the troops stationed in and around Washington under command of General Pope. Halleck went to see McClellan who told him that with 30,000 more troops he could take Richmond. He was offered 20,000, which number he accepted.

Yet, as soon as Halleck returned to Washington, a message arrived from McClellan asking not for 20,000 but for 40,000 reinforcements because—so he believed—the 90,000 men under his command were opposed by more than twice that number of Confederates. (In reality, during the entire duration of the war, General Lee's army never numbered more than 75,000.)

Lincoln was forced to make a decision. Understanding that the large Confederate army between McClellan and Pope was a potential menace to the Union forces, he ordered McClellan to leave the Peninsula and join up with Pope. McClellan angrily protested the order, but without avail.

When General Lee learned that McClellan was not going to receive reinforcements, he boldly moved an army against Pope, aiming to destroy his forces before McClellan's troops could reach him. Lincoln, the master strategist, guessed what Lee wanted to accomplish and implored McClellan to act fast.

McClellan as usual, took his time. On August 24 when the Confederates crossed the Rappahannock and threatened Pope from the rear McClellan was still far away. In a note he advised the President that if the forces could not join up, Pope should be left "to get out of his own scrape." It showed him at his worst— a General who seemed pleased at a rival's predicament. The callous remark shocked Lincoln.

On August 29 and 30 General Lee attacked and punished Pope in the second Battle of Bull Run.

The defeat left the army disorganized, its discipline slack. Once more Lincoln was compelled to turn to McClellan. "I must have McClellan to reorganize the army," he confided to his Secretary of the Navy, "and bring it out of chaos, but there has been a design, a purpose in breaking down Pope, without regard of consequences to the country. It is shocking to see and know this; but there is no remedy at present. McClellan has the army with him." Little Mac was given the temporary command of the forces around Washington.

Lincoln had no illusions about him; he knew his shortcomings, his slowness, his egomania and arrogance. But he also knew that in a situation such as the army now found itself, McClellan was the best man to organize and train the troops.

And when Lee moved into Maryland a few days later, and the Union needed a field commander, it was once more McClellan. The exultant General wrote his wife: "Again I have been called upon to save the country. The case is desperate, but with God's help I will try unselfishly to do my best, and, if He wills it, accomplish the salvation of the nation."

This time luck was with him. An Indiana private found an order revealing the disposition of the Confederate forces. "Here is a paper," cried out Little Mac, "with which if I cannot whip 'Bobby Lee,' I will be willing to go home." A small preliminary skirmish he magnified into a resounding victory. And Lincoln answered: "God bless you, and all with you. Destroy the rebel army if possible." Two days later, on September 17, the forces of the Union and the Confederacy clashed at Antietam Creek in one of the bloodiest encounters of the war. Lee was forced to withdraw from the battlefield.

If McClellan had been daring, the Confederate army could have been destroyed at Antietam. But he was cautious; during the crucial time he kept a whole corps in reserve when they should have been ordered into the fighting, and when Lee retreated, he allowed him to escape without pursuit.

Lincoln, meditated on the fate of the armies:

"The will of God prevails. In great contests each party claims to act in accordance with the will of God. Both may be, and one must be, wrong. God cannot be for and against the same thing at the same time. In the present civil war it is quite possible that God's purpose is something different from the purpose of either party; and yet the human instrumentalities, working just as they do, are the best adaptation to effect his purpose. I am almost ready to say that this is probably true; that God wills this contest, and wills that it should not end yet. By his mere great power on the minds of the new contestants, he could have either saved or destroyed the Union without a human contest. Yet the contest began. And, having begun, he could give the final victory to either side any day. Yet the contest proceeds."

The day after he put these thoughts on paper, he went to see McClellan, spending four days with the army, sleeping in a tent at the General's headquarters. Early one morning as he walked through the rows of tents, he turned in despair to his Illinois friend Ozias M. Hatch: "Hatch, Hatch, what is all this?"

"It is the Army of the Potomac, Mr. President."

"No, Hatch, no. This is McClellan's body guard."

Lincoln asked the General to cross the Potomac and pursue the Confederates while the roads were still good. McClellan promised, but soon he reverted to his old behavior, asking for more men, more supplies, more horses. Lincoln prodded him: "Are you not over-cautious when you assume that you cannot do what the enemy is constantly doing? Should you not claim to be at least his equal in prowess, and act upon the claim?"

The President offered a plan. If Lee "should move northward, I would follow him closely, holding his communications. If he should prevent our seizing his communications and move toward Richmond, I would press closely to him, fight him if a favorable opportunity should present, and at least try to beat him to Richmond on the inside track. I say 'try'; if we never try, we shall never succeed. If he makes a stand at Winchester, moving neither north nor south, I would fight him there, on the idea that if we cannot beat him when he bears the wastage of coming to us, we never can when we bear the wastage of going to him. This proposition is a simple truth, and is too important, to be lost sight of for a moment. In coming to us he tenders us an advantage which we should not waive. We should not so operate as to merely drive him away. As we must beat him somewhere or fail finally, we can do it, if at all, easier near to us than far away. If we cannot beat the enemy where he now is, we never can . . ." Yet, when six weeks later McClellan crossed the Potomac, Lee was already out of reach.

On November 5 Lincoln relieved McClellan of his command. "I said I would remove him," he told a politician who came to intercede for the General, "if he let Lee's army get away from him, and I must do so. He has got the 'slows.'"

The new chief was thirty-eight-year-old Ambrose E. Burnside, a handsome, dashing and impetuous man with side whiskers. Within two days Burnside devised a plan proposing a move against Fredericksburg and from there to Richmond.

He left camp, moved to Falmouth and then toward Fredericksburg, only to stop at the Rappahannock for a full week, waiting for pontoons. And while he waited,

LINCOLN ASKS GENERAL McCLELLAN, who instead of pursuing Lee kept sending messages about sore-tongued and fatigued horses, "what the horses of your army have done since the battle of Antietam that fatigues anything?"

HIS WIFE. The earliest picture of Mary Todd (1818-1882). She met her future husband at a ball in 1839 and a three-year courtship followed, interrupted by quarrels, separations and reconciliations. They were married on November 4, 1842.

HIS STEPMOTHER
Sarah Bush Johnston (1788-
1869) as she looked in old age.
After Nancy Hanks' death in
1818, Thomas Lincoln made
Sarah Bush his second wife.
She proved a good mother to
his children. Lincoln said,
"All that I am, or hope to be,
I owe to my angel mother."

HIS SWEETHEART
Mary Owens (1808-1877), a
tall, portly girl weighing
170 pounds, turned down his
marriage offer, explaining
later: "Mr. Lincoln was deficient in those little links
which make up the chain of
a woman's happiness — at
least it was so in my case."

HIS FIRST PARTNER
John Todd Stuart (1807-1885), one of the Whig leaders in Illinois, encouraged Lincoln to study law and offered him a partnership.

HIS COUSIN
Dennis Hanks (1799-1892), a natural son of an aunt of Nancy Hanks, who lived with the Lincolns after his foster parents died. Later he married Elizabeth, the eldest daughter of Sarah Johnston. Dennis lived to be 93, and in his old age he told many incidents of Lincoln's youth.

★

HIS LAST PARTNER
William Henry Herndon (1818-1891), Lincoln's third law partner. Not long after the President's assassination Herndon set himself the tremendous task of gathering all available material on Lincoln's life, subsequently used in his famous biography.

163

THE CHILDREN (left to right): Robert Todd, b. August 1, 1843; William Wallace, b. December 21, 1850; the same year four-year-old Eddie died; Thomas (Tad), b. April 4, 1853.

BEFORE LEAVING SPRINGFIELD in 1861, Mary Todd Lincoln posed with Willie and Tad for a daguerreotypist.

On the left: **LINCOLN WITH HIS SON TAD,** taken in Mathew B. Brady's Washington studio on February 9, 1864.

HIS POLITICAL RIVAL: Stephen A. Douglas (1813-1861), the Democratic Senator of Illinois, introduced the Kansas-Nebraska Act in 1854. The repeal of the Missouri Compromise aroused Lincoln "as he had never been before." He returned to the political arena, four years later opposing Douglas in the Illinois senatorial contest. This campaign and his debates made his name known over the nation and were vital stepping stones to his presidential nomination

WITH HIS SECRETARIES: (left) John George Nicolay (1832-1901), and John Hay (1838-1905). A photograph taken by Alexander Gardner less than a fortnight before Lincoln went to Gettysburg to deliver his immortal address. About ten years after the President's death Nicolay and Hay began their collaboration on their monumental work, *Abraham Lincoln: A History*. For fifteen years they toiled, publishing their ten-volume biography in 1890.

MARY LINCOLN READY FOR THE BALL. She disliked having her picture taken. "My hands are always made in them, very large and I look too stern." Because of the great difference in height, she never posed with her husband.

"WHERE ARE MY 15,000 SONS—murdered at Fredericksburg?" Columbia demands of the President in this bitter *Harper's Weekly* cartoon of January 1863. And Lincoln is pictured as saying: "This reminds me of a little joke."

Lee brought up his reinforcements. Thus, on December 13, when Burnside ordered the attack, the Confederates held entrenched positions on the heights above the city. Before nightfall the losses of the Union mounted to 12,000 men.

The tragic reverse at Fredericksburg incited the North. The President's handling of the war came under severe attack. Lincoln was desperate. "We are on the brink of destruction," he said to a friend. "It appears to me the Almighty is against us and I can hardly see a ray of hope."

In January 1863 Burnside's resignation was accepted; the General's quarrels with other high-ranking officers made his dismissal unavoidable.

He was replaced with handsome Joseph Hooker, "a gay cavalier, alert and confident, overflowing with animal spirits, and as cheery as a boy." Lincoln asked him to his study and handed him this letter:

LINCOLN'S FAMOUS LETTER TO HOOKER in 1863 after he had appointed the General to the command: "General. I have placed you at the head of the Army of the Potomac. Of course I have done this upon what appear to me to be sufficient reasons. And yet I think it best for you to know that there are some things in regard to which, I am not quite satisfied with you. I believe you to be a brave and a skilful soldier, which, of course, I like. I also believe you do not mix politics with your profession, in which you are right. You have confidence in yourself, which is a valuable, if not an indispensable quality. You are ambitious, which, within reasonable bounds, does good rather than harm. . . .

170

"I have heard, in such a way as to believe it, of your recently saying that both the Army and the Government needed a Dictator. Of course it was not *for* this, but in spite of it, that I have given you the command. Only those generals who gain successes, can set up dictators. What I now ask of you is military success, and I will risk the dictatorship. The government will support you to the utmost of it's ability, which is neither more nor less than it has done and will do for all commanders . . .

"And now, beware of rashness. Beware of rashness, but with energy, and sleepless vigilance, go forward, and give us victories."

At the beginning of May the Army of the Potomac was once more advancing toward Fredericksburg. Near the village of Chancellorville a battle was fought —another great defeat for the Union.

As Lincoln learned the news of the disaster, his face turned ashen. Pacing his room he moaned: "My God! My God! What will the country say! What will the country say!"

That very afternoon Hooker came to Washington. The President gave him a note of advice. "If possible I would be very glad of another movement early enough to give us some benefit from the fact of the enemy's communications being broken, but neither for this reason or any other, do I wish anything done in desperation or rashness," Lincoln wrote. "An early movement would also help to supersede the bad moral effect of the recent one, which is sure to be considerably injurious. Have you already in your mind a plan wholly, or partially formed? If you have, prossecute [sic] it without interference from me. If you have not, please inform me, so that I, incompetent as I may be, can try to assist in the formation of some plan for the Army."

But a month later, when the General planned to cross the Rappahannock and attack the rear of the Confederates, Lincoln warned him:

"I would not take any risk of being entangled upon the river, like an ox jumped half over the fence, and liable to be torn by dogs, front and rear, without a fair chance to gore one way or kick the other. If Lee would come to my side of the river, I would keep on the same side and fight him, or act on the defense, according as might be my estimate of his strength relatively [sic] to my own."

As Lee moved forward, the best strategy was to

follow him and attack when time and place were advantageous. Lincoln detected the flaw in Lee's plan and wrote to Hooker: "If the head of Lee's army is at Martinsburg and the tail of it on the plank road between Fredericksburg and Chancellorsville, the animal must be very slim somewhere. Could you not break him?"

But with every day Hooker behaved more like McClellan—demanding more troops and more supplies. His nerves on edge, he quarreled with General Halleck and threatened resignation. Lincoln had to choose between Halleck and Hooker—and he chose Halleck. On June 28—as a battle was shaping up—Hooker was relieved of his command; and in his stead the President named General George Meade, "the old snapping turtle," a methodical man with a short temper, stern and solemn, without humor or wit, but with a gift for military tactics.

Under Meade, on the first three days of July, the greatest single engagement of the Civil War was fought at the little town of Gettysburg, Pennsylvania. It was a great defeat for the South, a turning of the tide for the North. The Confederates retreated, leaving thousands of their best men on the battlefield.

On July 4, a day after Gettysburg, came news from General Grant that he had taken Vicksburg. The Mississippi was free. Lincoln said hopefully: "Now, if General Meade can complete his work, so gloriously prosecuted thus far, by the literal or substantial destruction of Lee's army, the rebellion will be over."

But when the President read Meade's congratulations to his troops, that the Union army must "drive from our soil every vestige of the presence of the invader," his hopes sank. "Drive the invader from our soil. My God! Is that all? Will our generals never . . . get that idea out of their heads? The whole country is our soil."

Meade was to go after Lee and destroy him before he crossed the Potomac. When Meade failed to move, Lincoln remarked that the General would "be ready to fight a magnificent battle when there is no enemy to fight." It was as he predicted. Lee had escaped. "We had them within our grasp. We had only to stretch forth our hands and they were ours."

General Halleck told Meade of the President's disappointment, in reply Meade offered his resignation. Lincoln penned a long letter, a letter which he never sent. "I do not believe you appreciate the magnitude of the misfortune involved in Lee's escape," he wrote. "He was within your easy grasp, and to have closed upon him would, in connection with our other late successes, have ended the war. As it is, the war will be prolonged indefinitely."

But another note was dispatched, a letter thanking General Ulysses S. Grant for what he had done. That letter read:

"I do not remember that you and I ever met personally. I write this now as a grateful acknowledgment for the almost inestimable service you have done the country. I wish to say a word further. When you first reached the vicinity of Vicksburg, I thought you should do, what you finally did—march the troops across the neck, run the batteries with the transports, and thus go below; and I never had any faith, except a general hope that you knew better than I, that the Yazoo Pass expedition, and the like, could succeed. When you got below, and took Port Gibson, Grand Gulf, and vicinity, I thought you should go down the river and join Gen. Banks; and when you turned northward East of the Big Black I feared it was a mistake. I now wish to make the personal acknowledgment that you were right, and I was wrong."

During the time General Grant was besieging Vicks-

Executive Mansion,
Washington. July 13, 1863.

Major General Grant
  My dear General

I do not remember that you and I ever met personally. I write this now as a grateful acknowledgment for the almost inestimable service you have done the country. I wish to say a word further. When you first reached the vicinity of Vicksburg, I thought you should do, what you finally did — march the troops across the neck, run the batteries with the transports, and thus go below; and I never had any faith, except a general hope that you knew better than I, that the Yazoo Pass expedition, and the like, could succeed. When you got below, and took Port-Gibson, Grand Gulf, and vicinity, I thought you should go down the river and join Gen. Banks; and when you turned Northward East of the Big Black, I feared it was a mistake. I now wish to make the personal acknowledgment that you were right, and I was wrong.
          Yours very truly
                A. Lincoln

AFTER THE CAPTURE OF VICKSBURG Lincoln thanks Grant "for the almost inestimable service you have done the country," and admits that he never had any faith in the success of the General's plan. "I now wish to make the personal acknowledgment that you were right, and I was wrong."

burg, Lincoln confided to an officer that if the General took that city, he "is my man and I am his the rest of the war." Now Grant had taken Vicksburg. After McClellan, Burnside, Hooker, Meade, the President had at last found his General.

.7 Emancipation Proclamation

One of Lincoln's cherished ideas was to offer financial aid to states that would take measures toward gradual, compensated emancipation. He argued that a single million dollars, or less than one-half day's cost of the war, would buy all the slaves in Delaware at $400 a head. Congress passed such a resolution without the votes of the border-state representatives.

As the war went on, the problem of emancipation became a burning question. How should the Negroes who flocked to the Northern camps be treated? Should they be used as laborers on the fortifications? Should they be allowed to do duty behind the lines?

As we know, in 1861, when General Frémont issued his proclamation freeing the slaves in his territory, Lincoln revoked the order. A year later, when General Hunter, in command of the Department of the South, proclaimed freedom for all slaves in Georgia, South Carolina and Florida, Lincoln again felt compelled to cancel the proclamation. "No commanding general shall do such a thing, upon *my* responsibility, without consulting me," he said.

The emancipation of the slaves was a political weapon, wrought of danger. It could have precipitated a break in the critical slave-holding border States still loyal to the Union. It could have dangerously antagonized those Democrats and conservative Republicans who were behind the government as long as it fought for the preservation of the Union, but would not support it if the object of the war became the elimination of slavery.

In July, 1862, the President was ready with a document proclaiming the freedom of the slaves in the rebellious states. When he read it to the Cabinet, the

Secretary of State pointed out that if such proclamation were issued in the wake of military defeats, the people would think that "the government is stretching forth its hands to Ethiopia, instead of Ethiopia stretching forth her hands to the government." Lincoln listened to Seward and decided to wait for a military victory.

In August the ever worrying Horace Greeley wrote to Senator Charles Sumner: "Do you remember that old theological book containing this: 'Chapter One—Hell; Chapter Two—Hell Continued.' Well, that gives a hint of the way Old Abe *ought to be* talked to in this crisis of the nation's destiny." Greeley, with other anti-slavery Republicans, opposed Lincoln's plan of compensated emancipation and was wrought up because the President was not taking the bold step of freeing the slaves.

In his open letter, "The Prayer of Twenty Millions," Greeley berated the President for being servile to the border-state politicians, who made him forget that "slavery is everywhere the inciting cause and sustaining base of treason."

Lincoln could have answered that he had already decided upon emancipation, that he had already written a proclamation, and that he was only waiting for the appropriate moment to announce it. Instead, he wrote Greeley: "My paramount object in this struggle *is* to save the Union, and is *not* either to save or to destroy slavery. If I could save the Union without freeing *any* slaves I would do it, and if I could save it by freeing *all* the slaves I would do it; and if I could save it by freeing some and leaving others alone would also do that."

But when—in September—the Battle of Antietam was won, Lincoln called his Cabinet together and told the Secretaries that the time had come to issue the proclamation. "What I have written is that which my reflections have determined me to say. If there is anything in the expressions I use, or in any other minor matter, which any one of you thinks had best be changed, I shall be glad to receive the suggestions. One other observation I will make. I know very well that many others might, in this matter, as in others, do better than I can; and if I were satisfied that the public confidence was more fully possessed by any one of them than by me, and knew of any Constitutional way in which he could be put in my place, he should have it. I would gladly yield it to him. But though I believe that I have not so much of the confidence of the people as I had some time since, I do not know that, all things considered, any other person has more; and, however this may be, there is no way in which I can have any other man put where I am. I am here. I must do the best I can, and bear the responsibility of taking the course which I feel I ought to take."

As Lincoln read to the Cabinet "That, on the first day of January, in the year of our Lord one thousand eight hundred and sixty-three, all persons held as slaves within any State or designated part of a State, the people whereof shall then be in rebellion against the United States, shall be then, thenceforward, and forever FREE; and the Executive Government of the United States, including the military and naval authority thereof, will *recognize* the freedom of such persons, and will do no act or acts to repress such persons, or any of them in any efforts they may make for their actual freedom," the Secretary of State interrupted him.

"I think Mr. President," said Seward, "that you should insert after the word '*recognize*,' in that sentence, the words '*and maintain*.'" Lincoln agreed.

On September 22, 1862, the preliminary Emancipation Proclamation was issued.

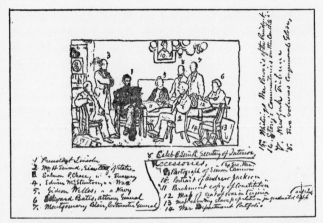

EMANCIPATION PROCLAMATION. Francis B. Carpenter's sketch for the painting, which now hangs in the Capitol.

A few weeks later, in his annual message to Congress, the President commented on his measure with eloquent words:

"Fellow-citizens, *we* cannot escape history. We of this Congress and this administration, will be remembered in spite of ourselves. No personal significance, or insignificance, can spare one or another of us. The fiery trial, through which we pass, will light us down, in honor, or dishonor, to the latest generation. We *say* we are for the Union. The world will not forget that we say this. We know how to save the Union. The world knows we do know how to save it. We—even *we here* —hold the power, and bear the responsibility. In *giving* freedom to the *slave*, we *assure* freedom to the *free*— honorable alike in what we give, and what we preserve. We shall nobly save, or meanly lose, the last, best hope of earth. Other means may succeed, this could not fail. The way is plain, peaceful, generous, just—a way which, if followed, the world will forever applaud, and God must forever bless."

On New Year's Day 1863, the final proclamation reached the public, freeing the slaves in the rebellious states. One must bear in mind that the Emancipation Proclamation freed the slaves only in the areas where the National Government as yet had no authority. "Yet it was nevertheless an immortal blow for human freedom," said Professor Nevins. "It not only changed the aims of the war, but it raised them to a higher level. Infusing a new moral meaning into the conflict, it deepened that element of passion and inspiration which vibrated in so many of Lincoln's utterances. It rallied the liberal thought of Britain and the globe to the Union side."

The reaction to the measure was highly critical. Abolitionists and Radical Republicans found it not far-reaching enough; while pro-slavery Democrats assailed the President, who had called upon the North to enter the struggle for the Union, when all he desired—as his proclamation showed—was to destroy slavery.

Lincoln, keeping his finger on the public pulse, saw that the measure was not well received.

The discontent against the government grew; secret societies sprung up agitating against the President advocating a negotiated peace; recruiting officers were murdered, loyal supporters harassed.

The Copperheads—the name given to those in the North who opposed the war and sympathized with the South—fomented the discontent. Clement L. Vallancigham, one of the leaders of the group was arrested and imprisoned. Lincoln, however, commuted his sentence to banishment behind the Confederate lines. Assailed by the opposition as an enemy of free speech, the President replied: "Must I shoot a simple-minded soldier boy who deserts, while I must not touch a hair of the wiley (sic) agitator who induces him to desert?"

With off-year elections approaching, Lincoln wrote

a letter to his friend James C. Conkling to be read at the Springfield meeting of the National Union party. Called "his last stump speech," it appealed to the dubious, it tried to convince the critical about the rightness of the administration's course.

"There are those who are dissatisfied with me. To such I would say: You desire peace; and you blame me that we do not have it. But how can we attain it? There are but three conceivable ways. First, to suppress the rebellion by force of arms. This, I am trying to do. Are you for it? If you are, so far we are agreed. If you are not for it, a second way is, to give up the Union. I am against this. Are you for it? If you are, you should say so plainly. If you are not for *force*, nor yet for *dissolution*, there only remains some imaginable *compromise*. I do not believe any compromise, embracing the maintenance of the Union, is now possible. All I learn, leads to a directly opposite belief."

And after arguing that "no paper compromise, to which the controllers of Lee's army are not agreed," could be effective, the President came to the vital point: "But, to be plain, you are dissatisfied with me about the negro. Quite likely there is a difference of opinion between you and myself upon that subject. I certainly wish that all men could be free, while I suppose you do not. Yet, I have neither adopted, nor proposed any measure, which is not consistent with even your view, provided you are for the Union. I suggested compensated emancipation; to which you replied you wished not to be taxed to buy negroes. But I had not asked you to be taxed to buy negroes, except in such way as to save you from greater taxation to save the Union exclusively by other means.

"You dislike the emancipation proclamation; and perhaps, would have it retracted. You say it is unconstitutional—I think differently. I think the Constitution invests its commander-in-chief, with the law of war, in time of war. The most that can be said, if so much, is, that slaves are property. Is there—has there ever been—any question that by the law of war, property, both of enemies and friends, may be taken when needed? And is it not needed whenever taking it, helps us, or hurts the enemy? . . .

"But the proclamation, as law, either is valid or is not valid. If it is not valid, it needs no retraction. If it is valid, it cannot be retracted, any more than the dead can be brought to life. Some of you profess to think its retraction would operate favorably for the Union. Why better *after* the retraction than *before* the issue? There was more than a year and a half of trial to suppress the rebellion before the proclamation issued; the last one hundred days of which passed under an explicit notice that it was coming, unless averted by those in revolt, returning to their allegiance. The war has certainly progressed as favorably for us, since the issue of the proclamation as before. I know as fully as one can know the opinions of others, that some of the commanders of our armies in the field who have given us our most important successes, believe the emancipation policy, and the use of colored troops, constitute the heaviest blow yet dealt to the rebellion, and that, at least one of those important successes, could not have been achieved when it was, but for the aid of black soldiers. Among the commanders holding these views are some who have never had any affinity with what is called abolitionism, or with republican party politics; but who hold them purely as military opinions. I submit these opinions as being entitled to some weight against the objections, often urged, that emancipation, and arming the blacks, are unwise as military measures, and were not adopted as such in good faith.

"You say you will not fight to free negroes. Some

of them seem willing to fight for you; but, no matter. Fight you, then, exclusively to save the Union. I issued the proclamation on purpose to aid you in saving the Union. Whenever you shall have conquered all resistance to the Union, if I shall urge you to continue fighting, it will be an apt time, then, for you to declare you will not fight to free negroes."

And the President concluded his message: "Peace does not appear so distant as it did. I hope it will come soon, and come to stay; and so come as to be worth the keeping in all future time. It will then have been proved that, among free men there can be no successful appeal from the ballot to the bullet; and that they who take such appeal are sure to lose their case, and pay the cost. And then, there will be some black men who can remember that, with silent tongue, and clenched teeth, and steady eye, and well-poised bayonet, they have helped mankind on to this great consummation; while, I fear there will be some white ones, unable to forget that, with malignant heart, and deceitful speech they strove to hinder it."

Lincoln's arguments swayed many minds. The opponents of the administration were soundly beaten. The Union ticket carried all the Northern states but New Jersey. In Ohio, Clement Vallandigham, the Copperhead Democrat, who called upon the voters of the State to defeat Lincoln's tyranny and make peace with the South, lost the Governorship to his opponent by more than 100,000 votes. Lincoln cried out in joy: "Glory to God in the highest. Ohio has saved the nation."

8. The Gettysburg Address

On November 19, 1863, the dedication of the Gettysburg National Cemetery was to take place. At first the committee organizing the ceremonies had not asked

Executive Mansion,

Washington,   186

Four score and seven years ago our fathers brought forth, upon this continent, a new nation, conceived in liberty, and dedicated to the proposition that "all men are created equal"

Now we are engaged in a great civil war, testing whether that nation, or any nation so conceived, and so dedicated, can long endure. We are met on a great battle field of that war. We have come to dedicate a portion of it, as a final resting place for those who died here that the nation might live. This we may, in all propriety do. But, in a larger sense, we can not dedicate— we can not consecrate— we can not hallow, this ground— The brave men, living and dead, who struggled here, have hallowed it, far above our poor power to add or detract. The world will little note, nor long remember what we say here; while it can never forget what they did here.

It is rather for us, the living, to stand here,

THE FIRST DRAFT OF THE GETTYSBURG ADDRESS: the first page written in ink, the second in pencil. At least six copies were made of the address, each slightly different

the President to make an address, as the gentlemen of that august body doubted whether he could "speak upon such a great and solemn occasion." But when he was belatedly invited "to set apart formally these grounds to their sacred use by a few appropriate remarks," he responded willingly.

He prepared his speech with great care. The story that he composed it while riding in the train to the

in length. The first draft had but 239 words, the last, 272. Most of the words used were short: 204 were of a single syllable each, 50 of two syllables, and only 18 of three or more.

ceremonies is a legend. The address was written in Washington and was revised often. Even after Lincoln arrived in Gettysburg, he reworked the speech. It was not till midnight that he had finished his task and walked over to Secretary Seward's lodging, where he read to Seward the final draft.

Next day more than fifteen thousand people came to the cemetery to hear Edward Everett, the foremost orator, the principal speaker at the ceremonies. Everett's booming voice kept the audience enthralled for two solid hours; his gestures underlined with dramatic effect the classical allusions of his oratory.

During Everett's speech the President kept looking at his manuscript, reading and rereading the two pages. And when Everett finished and Lincoln rose to his feet, he held his manuscript tightly with both hands. As he began to speak, his voice sounded shrill:

"Four score and seven years ago, our fathers brought forth on this continent, a new nation, conceived in Liberty, and dedicated to the proposition that all men are created equal." The words could be clearly heard on the field where restless listeners were wandering about.

"Now we are engaged in a great civil war, testing whether that nation, or any nation so conceived and so dedicated, can long endure. We are met on a great battle-field of that war. We have come to dedicate a portion of that field, as a final resting place for those who here gave their lives that that nation might live. It is altogether fitting and proper that we should do this."

To the people before the platform the unembellished phrases, the simple language of the President seemed flat after Everett's flowery oratory.

"But, in a larger sense, we cannot dedicate—we cannot consecrate—we cannot hallow—this ground. The brave men, living and dead, who struggled here, have consecrated it, far above our poor power to add or detract. The world will little note, nor long remember what we say here, but it can never forget what they did here. It is for us the living, rather, to be dedicated here to the unfinished work which they who fought here have thus far so nobly advanced. It is rather for us to be here dedicated to the great task remaining before us—that from these honored dead we take increased devotion to that cause for which they gave the last full measure of devotion—that we here highly resolve that these dead shall not have died in vain—that this nation, under God, shall have a new birth of freedom—and that government of the people, by the people, for the people, shall not perish from the earth."

Thus the speech ended. Lincoln spoke for less than three minutes; a photographer before him had not the time to focus his lens, put a plate into his camera and release the shutter; the address was over almost before it began.

On the platform Edward Everett whispered to Secretary of State Seward: "It is not what I expected from him. I am disappointed." Seward, too, thought that the President had "made a failure. . . . His speech was not equal to him."

Lincoln himself felt badly about his address; he thought it did not "scour," and that it "fell on the audience like a wet blanket." He reproached himself later: "I ought to have prepared it with more care."

The newspapers too were unimpressed by the President's Gettysburg address. The nearby Harrisburg paper wrote: "We pass over the silly remarks of the President; for the credit of the nation we are willing that the veil of oblivion shall be dropped over them and that they shall no more be repeated or thought of." The correspondent of the London *Times* reported that "The ceremony was rendered ludicrous by some of the sallies of that poor President Lincoln, who seems determined to play, in this great American union the part of the famous Governor of Barataria. Anything more dull and commonplace it wouldn't be easy to produce."

The first favorable comment came from the Chicago *Tribune*, and was followed by the Springfield *Repub-*

lican, a Massachusetts paper. "Turn back and read it over," advised the *Republican*, "it will repay study as a model speech. Strong feelings and a large brain were its parents—a little painstaking, its accoucheur."

9. *Ebb Tide*

On the way back from Gettysburg, Lincoln fell mildly ill with smallpox; arriving at the Capital, all his interviews were canceled, the hordes of office seekers kept away. It was a pity, he joked, "I have something now that I can give to everybody."

While bedridden, the news came from General Grant that "Lookout Mountain Top, all the rifle pits in Chattanooga, and Missionary Ridge entire, have been carried and now held by us." The defeat of the Confederates in Georgia was complete.

Grant, the son of the Illinois tanner, Grant, the hard-drinking, determined, reticent man, Grant, the scrubby-looking little man with a rough-whiskered face and penetrating eyes, was the hero of the day. The cry went up to appoint him as head of the army, and the President complied happily.

In March, 1864, Ulysses S. Grant, the new Lieutenant General, journeyed to Washington to accept the honor, and President and General met for the first time. Lincoln told him that he could plan his strategy without fear of any interference and revealed to the General that "he had never professed to be a military man or to know how campaigns should be conducted, and never wanted to interfere with them; but that procrastination on the part of commanders, and pressure from the people at the North and Congress, which was always with him, forced him into issuing his series of 'Military orders'—one, two, three, etc. He did not know but they were all wrong, and did know that some

DON QUIXOTE AND SANCHO PANZA. A caricature etching by Adalbert J. Volck of Baltimore, showing Don Quixote Lincoln with his shrewd servant Sancho Panza, one of the best-hated men in the South: General Benjamin F. Butler.

of them were. All he wanted or had ever wanted was some one who would take the responsibility and act, and call on him for all the assistance needed, pledging himself to the use of all the power of the Government in rendering such assistance."

The President had confidence in the new commander-in-chief. Grant was single-minded in his desire to bring the struggle to a victorious and speedy end.

His plan was to use all the troops at his disposal and to harass and wear the Confederacy down. He proposed three major movements to be executed at the same time. Meade, with the Army of the Potomac, was to attack Lee; Butler, with the Army of the James, was to destroy Lee's communications and invest Richmond; Sherman, with the Army of the Tennessee, was to fight Johnston and move against Atlanta.

At the beginning of May the forward move began. To the President's good wishes, Grant replied tersely: "Should my success be less than I desire, and expect, the least I can say is, the fault is not with you."

The fighting in the Wilderness—as the region south of the Rapidan was called—lasted for many weeks. In the dense Virginia woods the two armies battled with desperate stubbornness. The Union had twice as many men as the Confederacy, but the terrain favored the latter. Union artillery had no effect in the thickly grown forest. The toll of death was tremendous; the Union lost 50,000 men, and yet the end was not in sight.

In the second week of June, after the bloody encounter at Cold Harbor, Grant shifted strategy. Withdrawing his troops from the outskirts of Richmond, he moved them to the south on the Peninsula and marched them from there toward Petersburg. He aimed to cut off Richmond from the rest of the Confederacy. Lincoln wired him: "I begin to see it; you will succeed. God bless you all."

But Lee stopped his adversary before Petersburg. To Grant's plan to make a "desperate effort" came the counsel from Lincoln: "Pressed as we are by lapse of time, I am glad to hear you say this; and yet I do hope you may find a way that the effort shall not be desperate in the sense of great loss of life."

The siege of the Confederate capital began. The Union army dug in before Petersburg. Grant had said that he would fight it out on that line "if it takes all summer." It did take all summer, and the winter as well. For nearly ten months—from June, 1864, till April, 1865—the army was in the trenches, mining and assaulting Lee's supply lines. Lincoln wired to Grant: "Hold on with a bulldog grip, and chew and choke as much as possible."

July and August, 1864, were the darkest months in the war. The people were weary of the struggle, tired of the war, tired of the continuous sacrifice. For the campaign in the Wilderness—costing so many lives— the President was blamed and assailed with renewed fervor.

Once more Horace Greeley berated him for not attempting to bring peace through negotiations. To Greeley's note about the Confederate emissaries who were supposed to be waiting on the Canadian side of Niagara Falls to parley, the President replied: "If you can find any person anywhere professing to have any proposition of Jefferson Davis in writing, for peace, embracing the restoration of the Union and abandonment of slavery . . . say to him he may come to me with you." And when Greeley sent another note of advice, the President answered curtly: "I was not expecting you to *send* me a letter but to *bring* me a man, or *men*." Lincoln put Greeley on the spot. He told him: "I not only intend a sincere effort for peace, but I intend that you shall be a personal witness that it is made." Thus Greeley left for Niagara Falls, only to find that the Confederate emissaries had no authority to speak for the South.

The Radical Republicans in Congress, using the general dissatisfaction against the President, passed a bill nullifying Lincoln's amnesty and reconstruction plan. At the beginning of December, 1863, Lincoln issued a proclamation. In it he proposed to give full pardon to persons taking part in the rebellion on the condition that they were ready to take an oath of loyalty to the Constitution and swear to support the Emancipation Proclamation and all acts of Congress dealing with slaves. The President promised that "whenever, in any of the States of Arkansas, Texas, Louisiana, Mississippi, Tennessee, Alabama, Georgia, Florida, South Carolina, and North Carolina, a number of persons, not less than one-tenth in number of the votes cast in such State at the Presidential election" of 1860, re-establish a democratic government, that government "shall be recognized as the true government of the State" and would receive Federal protection against invasion and against domestic violence.

However, the bill of the Radical Republicans, known as the Wade-Davis bill, required that not ten per cent, but a majority of the voters must declare themselves loyal to the Union before the seceded state could be taken back into the fold, and that no one who had held Confederate office or who had voluntarily borne arms against the United States should be allowed to vote. Furthermore, the constitutions of the restored states must prohibit slavery and repudiate the "rebel" debt.

Pocketing the radicals' bill, Lincoln declared that he would neither set aside the free state constitutions and governments of Louisiana and Arkansas, nor would he acknowledge that Congress had the power to abolish slavery in the states.

The radicals replied with a manifesto denouncing the President's reconstruction policies and charging that he had only recognized the governments in Arkansas and Louisiana because he needed their votes for his re-election. Lincoln felt the sting deeply. To a newspaper friend he complained: "To be wounded in the house of one's friends is perhaps the most grievous affliction that can befall a man."

10. *Re-elected*

On October 12, 1863, Elihu B. Washburne, Congressman from Illinois, wrote the President: "Notwithstand-

Lorant No. 96

IN McCLELLAN'S TENT at Antietam. On October 2, 1862, the President visited the Commander of the Armies to urge him to take advantage of his victory and pursue the Confederates. "Little Mac" was hesitant; Lincoln replaced him.

HIS GENERALS

WINFIELD SCOTT
(1786-1866), General-in-Chief
of the Army since 1841, a hero
of two wars, but in 1861 old
and infirm with dropsy and
vertigo. Resigned in October.

GEORGE B. McCLELLAN
(1826-1885) succeeded Scott.
A brilliant organizer, but hesitant when it came to action.
After Antietam Lincoln relieved him of his command.

AMBROSE E. BURNSIDE
(1824-1881) succeeded McClellan as Commander of the
Army of the Potomac on Nov.
5, 1862. Dashing and brave, but
a poor planner and leader.

JOSEPH HOOKER
(1814-1879) relieved Burnside
in January 1863 after the disaster at Fredericksburg.
"Fighting Joe" resigned following defeat at Chancellorsville.

GEORGE G. MEADE
(1815-1872) succeeded Hooker
on June 28, 1863. Efficient and
studious, he won the decisive
battle of Gettysburg, but failed
to follow up his advantage.

ULYSSES S. GRANT
(1822-1885) became Lieuten-
ant-General of the Army in
1864. In him Lincoln at last had
found a general who was able to
give victories and end the war.

HENRY W. HALLECK
(1815-1872) became Lincoln's
military advisor in July 1862
and titled General-in-Chief.
Under Grant, "Old Brain"
Halleck was Chief of Staff.

WILLIAM T. SHERMAN
(1820-1891) was named Commander of the Armies of the
West when Grant became
Chief of the Army. Later Sherman said: "War . . . is all hell."

195

HIS CABINET

WILLIAM H. SEWARD
(1801-1872), Secretary of State. A former governor and senator of New York, he was Lincoln's chief rival for the presidential nomination in Chicago.

SALMON P. CHASE
(1808-1873), Secretary of the Treasury until July 1864, when he became Chief Justice. Pompous and egotistical, he never recognized Lincoln's genius.

GIDEON WELLES
(1802-1878), Secretary of the Navy, a former Democrat from Connecticut. Wearing a wavy beard and a blonde wig, he resembled Father Neptune.

SIMON CAMERON
(1799-1899), Lincoln's first Secretary of War. A political boss from Pennsylvania, he received the Cabinet post as the result of a convention bargain.

EDWIN M. STANTON (1814-1869), Secretary of War from January 15, 1862. Able, energetic and honest, but arbitrary, tactless and disagreeable, he once referred to Lincoln as the "original gorilla." But he served the President with devotion.

197

CALEB B. SMITH
(1808-1864), Secretary of the Interior until the end of 1862. At the Republican convention he was promised a Cabinet post for the votes of Indiana.

JOHN P. USHER
(1816-1889), Secretary of the Interior from January 1863; who succeeded Caleb Smith. A good administrator, greatly interested in public land policies.

MONTGOMERY BLAIR
(1813-1883), Postmaster General. A member of the influential political family, counsel for the slave Dred Scott, an ardent Unionist from Maryland.

WILLIAM DENNISON
(1815-1882), Postmaster General after Blair's resignation in 1864. An aristocratic, unpopular businessman, Governor of Ohio when Civil War began.

HUGH McCULLOCH
(1808-1895) Secretary of the Treasury, following Fessenden. A successful banker, he took over the cabinet post not long before the end of the Civil War.

WILLIAM P. FESSENDEN
(1806-1869), Secretary of the Treasury after Chase became Chief Justice. He resigned in 1865 when Maine elected him for third time to the Senate.

EDWARD BATES
(1793-1869), Attorney General, the first Cabinet member to be chosen from the land west of the Mississippi. Opposing Lincoln he resigned in 1864.

JAMES SPEED
(1812-1887), Attorney General who succeeded Bates. A conservative Southerner, he was Lincoln's devoted friend from his early Springfield days.

199

ANDREW JOHNSON
(1808-1875), Vice-
President elected with
Lincoln in 1864. A
Jacksonian Democrat
from the South, for ten
successive years he
represented Tennessee
in the House of Rep-
resentatives, then was
elected to the Senate.
In 1862 was his state's
Military Governor.

★

HANNIBAL HAMLIN
(1809-1891), Vice
President elected with
Lincoln in 1860. A
former Democrat,
Governor and Senator
from Maine, he was a
strongly anti-slavery
man and a firm advo-
cate of Emancipation.

ing the troubles that surround us, the time has come when we must confront the question of our next presidential candidate. I think you ought to let some of your confidential friends know your wishes." And Lincoln answered: "A second term would be a great honor and a great labor, which together, perhaps I would not decline, if tendered."

He desired a second term to complete the task he had begun; end the war, restore the Union and bring the seceded states back under the flag without rancor and discrimination. Yet, as the year 1864 dawned the signs were dark; many of the most influential Republicans were opposed to a second term.

Salmon P. Chase, the Secretary of the Treasury, believed that "a man of different qualities from those of the President will be needed for the next four years," and assuming that he was just this kind of man, he allowed his friends to organize a movement in his behalf. Early in February, Senator Samuel C. Pomeroy of Kansas, a Chase supporter, issued a circular declaring that the cause of liberty and union would suffer by the President's re-election and that the salutary one-term principle, which since Andrew Jackson's election in 1832 had been faithfully observed in the United States, was a safeguard of Republican institutions. Pomeroy announced the formation of a central organization in order to allow Chase's friends "most effectually to promote his elevation to the Presidency."

When the contents of the privately distributed circular became known, the alarmed Chase denied any knowledge of it and offered his resignation. Lincoln replied: "Whether you shall remain at the head of the Treasury Department is a question which I will not allow myself to consider from any standpoint other than my judgment of the public service; and, in that view, I do not perceive occasion for a change."

THE 1864 PRESIDENTIAL CANDIDATES are reviewed by Uncle Sam. On the left, next to Lincoln, is General McClellan, the Democratic candidate; in the center, General Butler.

The circular, instead of hurting the President, helped him. His supporters closed ranks, and one after the other the various state conventions endorsed his renomination.

An arrogant group of Radical Republicans still believed they could frustrate his candidacy by proposing the postponement of the national convention, in the hope that reverses in the war might turn the country against the President. Horace Greeley asserted that not only Chase, but Frémont, Butler or Grant would make as good a President as Lincoln, and suggested nominating one of them to preserve the "salutory one-term principle" of the last three decades. As Butler had no real support and Grant would not take the nomination, Lincoln's enemies turned to General John C. Frémont, the Republican's presidential candidate of 1856. In a convention at Cleveland the "Radical Democracy" —as the dissident Republicans called themselves—he was chosen as their standard bearer. Frémont accepted the honor and orated that if the President were renominated, "there will remain no alternative but to organize against him every element of conscientious opposition with a view to prevent the misfortune of his reelection."

When Lincoln heard that only four hundred people were present at the Radical's convention, he laughed. Opening the Bible, he read the passage from Samuel: "And every one that was in distress, and every one that was in debt, and every one that was discontented, gathered themselves unto him; and he became a captain over them; and there were with him about four hundred men." A week later the National Unionists—the new temporary name of the Republicans—met in Baltimore and renominated Lincoln.

Replying to a delegation of the National Union League who came to offer their best wishes, the President said: "I do not allow myself to suppose that either the convention or the League have concluded to decide that I am either the greatest or best man in Amer-

WHO WILL FIT HIS SHOES? A cartoon from the time when the President's renomination was in doubt. Pigmy politicians are measuring Lincoln, the sleeping giant's boots.

Executive Mansion
Washington, Aug 23, 1864.

This morning, as for some days past, it seems exceedingly probable that this Administration will not be here-after, elected. Then it will be my duty to so co-operate with the President elect, as to save the Union between the election and the inauguration; as he will have secured his election on such ground that he cannot possibly save it afterwards.

A. Lincoln

HIS RE-ELECTION IN DOUBT, Lincoln asked the members of his cabinet to sign the above statement: "This morning, as for some days past, it seems exceedingly probable that this Administration will not be re-elected. Then it will be my duty to so co-operate with the President-elect as to save the

ica, but rather they have concluded it is not best to swap horses while crossing the river, and have further concluded that I am not so poor a horse that they might not make a botch of it in trying to swap."

But even Lincoln's official renomination did not end the movement against him. Republican newspapermen and politicians banded together in an attempt to force his withdrawal; they proposed to call a convention at Cincinnati to agree on a candidate who had the confidence of the country "even by a new nomination if necessary." Horace Greeley asserted: "Mr. Lincoln is already beaten. He cannot be elected. And we must

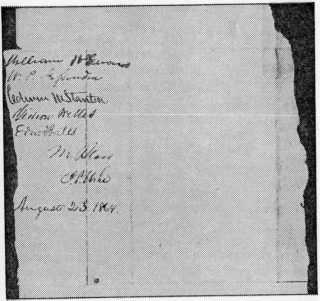

Union between the election and the inauguration, as he will have secured his election on such ground that he can not possibly save it afterwards." The sheet was folded over in such a way that its contents could not be read. Only after the election did the Secretaries learn what they had signed.

have another ticket to save us from overthrow. If we had such a ticket as could be made by naming Grant, Butler or Sherman for President, and Farragut for Vice, we could make a fight yet. And such a ticket we ought to have anyhow, with or without a convention."

The Lincoln men were in an uneasy mood. The military failures and heavy casualties of the Wilderness Campaign dismayed the country. Sherman's army was bogged down before Atlanta. Henry J. Raymond, the editor of the New York *Times* and chairman of the Republican National Committee, told Lincoln bluntly: "The tide is against us." And he reported that "the

THE DEMOCRATIC CANDIDATE, George B. McClellan, pictured as Hamlet, looks at his rival's head and exclaims: "I knew him, Horatio, a fellow of infinite jest . . ."

THE TRUE ISSUE. A Currier and Ives cartoon from August 1864, in which McClellan holds Lincoln and Jeff Davis abreast. Lincoln says: "No peace without abolition." Jefferson Davis: "No peace without separation," while McClellan exclaims: "The Union must be preserved at all hazards."

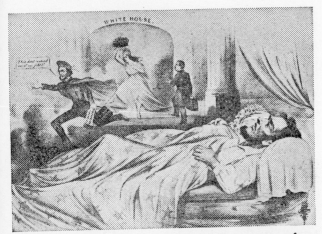

ABRAHAM'S DREAM. A Currier and Ives cartoon from October 1864, in which the Goddess of Liberty is driving Lincoln from the White House, while McClellan ascends.

THE RAILSPLITTER AT WORK. A cartoon drawn by Baker for Currier and Ives a month after Lincoln's renomination for the second term. The President says to Vice-President Andrew Johnson, the former tailor: "A few more stitches, Andy, and the good old Union will be mended."

suspicion is widely diffused that we can have peace with Union if we would." Therefore, Raymond proposed the appointment of a peace commission to negotiate with the Confederate government. If Jefferson Davis would acknowledge the supremacy of the Constitution, all other issues could be settled by a convention in which both North and South were represented.

The President prepared himself for defeat. A week before the Democrats met in their nominating convention, and when it was common knowledge that their candidate would be General McClellan, Lincoln penned on a piece of paper: "This morning, as for some days past, it seems exceedingly probable that this Administration will not be re-elected. Then it will be my duty to so co-operate with the President-elect, as to save the Union between the election and the inauguration; as he will have secured his election on such ground that he can not possibly save it afterward." Without letting the Cabinet see what he had written, he asked the members

---

A. LINCOLN,

Attorney and Counsellor at Law,

SPRINGFIELD, ILL.

TO WHOM IT MAY CONCERN

My old customers and others are no doubt aware of the terrible time I have had in *crossing the stream*, and will be glad to know that I will be back on the same side from which I started on or before the 4TH OF MARCH next. when I will be ready to *Swap Horses, Dispense Law, Make Jokes. Split Rails*, and perform other matters in a SMALL way.

A CAMPAIGN CARD of 1864 ridiculing Lincoln's remark that he was renominated because his supporters had "concluded it is not best to swap horses while crossing the river."

THE ELECTORAL VOTE. In a pre-election tally Lincoln jotted down the number of electors from the various states.

of his political family to endorse the document on the reverse side of the sheet.

He later explained to them why he had requested this. "I resolved, in case of the election of General Mc-Clellan, being certain that he would be the candidate, that I would see him and talk matters over with him. I would say, 'General, the election has demonstrated that you are stronger, have more influence with the American people than I. Now let us together, you with your influence and I with all the executive power of the government, try to save the country. You raise as

209

many troops as you possibly can for this final trial, and I will devote all my energies to assisting and finishing the war.' "

The platform of the Democrats declared that "after four years of failure to restore the Union by experiment of war . . . the public welfare demands that immediate efforts be made for a cessation of hostilities to the end that, at the earliest practicable moment, peace may be restored on the basis of the Federal Union of the States." To put these policies into effect the Democrats chose General George B. McClellan.

Little Mac accepted the nomination but refused the platform. "I could not look in the face of my gallant comrades of the army and navy," wrote he, "who have survived so many bloody battles, and tell them that their labors and the sacrifices of so many of our slain and wounded brethren had been in vain; that we had abandoned that Union for which we have so often perilled our lives." In McClellan's opinion: "No peace can be permanent without Union."

The Democratic Convention had hardly disbanded when the news broke that Sherman had taken Atlanta. This, paired with Admiral Farragut's triumph at Mobile Bay, turned the tide in Lincoln's favor. "Sherman and Farragut have knocked the bottom out of the Chicago nominations," exclaimed Seward. Now, the President's adversaries climbed on his band wagon. Chase came and made amends; Greeley, too, now silent about a negotiated peace, was back in the fold. The radicals withdrew Frémont as a candidate, and in return, Lincoln dropped from the Cabinet Montgomery Blair, who had long been a thorn in the radicals' flesh.

By October, Chase could say: "There is not now, the slightest uncertainty about the re-election of Mr. Lincoln. The only question is by what popular and electoral majority. God grant that both may be so

RE-ELECTED.
Frank Bellew called
his cartoon "Long
Abraham a little
longer." It appeared
in *Harper's Weekly*.

decisive as to turn every hope of rebellion to despair!"

Victory at the polls was a decisive one. Lincoln received 2,213,665 popular votes as against McClellan's 1,802,237. The soldier ballots, which were counted separately, favored the President with 116,877 votes as against McClellan's 33,748.

"I give you joy of the election," wrote Ralph Waldo Emerson to a friend. "Seldom in history was so much staked on a popular vote. I suppose never in history."

To the cheering crowd who came to serenade him, Lincoln said thoughtfully: "It has long been a grave question whether any government not too strong for the liberties of its people, can be strong enough to maintain its existence in great emergencies. On this point the present rebellion brought our republic to a severe test, and a Presidential election occurring in regular course during the rebellion, added not a little to the strain.

"If the loyal people united were put to the utmost of their strength by the rebellion, must they not fail when divided and partially paralyzed by a political war among themselves? But the election was a necessity. We cannot have free government without elections, and if the rebellion could force us to forego or postpone a national election, it might fairly claim to have already conquered and ruined us."

And the President renewed his thoughts: "The election, along with its incidental and undesirable strife, has done good too. It has demonstrated that a people's government can sustain a national election in the midst of a great civil war. Until now, it has not been known to the world that this was a possibility. It shows, also, how sound and how strong we still are."

He was confident of the future, confident that the nation would be soon united again. His faith shone brightly.

11. *His Day*

He rose early; by eight o'clock he was through with his breakfast—a cup of coffee, an egg and toast. Then he looked at his mail. His secretary John Hay recalled: "He wrote very few letters. He did not read one in fifty that he received. . . . He wrote perhaps half-a-dozen a week himself, not more." His official day began at ten o'clock, but the anterooms and halls were full long before that hour. At first he was seeing applicants at almost any time during the day, but when their number grew, the visiting period was limited to the hours from ten to three and later from ten to one. Yet Lincoln was not the man to observe such rules; he was unmethodical and unbusinesslike. His secretary recalled: "He would break through every regulation as fast as it was made. Anything that kept the people themselves away from him he disapproved—although they nearly annoyed the life out of him by unreasonable complaints and requests."

Cabinet members had first call on his time, then Senators and Representatives, who were more often than not accompanied by their constituents. On Tuesdays and Fridays the "public opinion baths" had to be cut short—these days the Cabinet met.

At noon he usually edged his way through the throng to his living-quarters, where he took a little lunch—biscuit, fruit and a glass of milk. Then—back for more work.

At four he drove out with Mary occasionally stopping at a hospital, where he chatted with wounded soldiers. He dined between five and six. He ate sparingly and cared little how the food was prepared. He drank no hard liquors, though occasionally he indulged in a glass of beer or wine. He never used tobacco.

Once a week—save in the summer months when the Lincolns stayed at the Soldiers' Home outside the city—an evening reception or levee was held in the White House with hundreds of guests present. On other evenings he was to be found at his desk. Before he turned into bed—which was usually between ten and eleven o'clock—he walked over to the War Department to read dispatches from the front. But if important battles had been fought, he remained in the telegraph office until the early hours of the morning.

Regularly friends came to visit him in the evening, and he read to them from Shakespeare or Robert Burns or from the works of contemporary humorists.

He liked music if it sounded sad and sentimental. Ward Hill Lamon often sang ballads for him, and he enjoyed the melodies of Stephen Foster. He was fond of the theater and of the opera. He needed the diversion. "I must have a change of some sort or die," he said.

He did not sleep well, but stayed in bed long hours. His little son Tad usually slept with him. In the evenings the boy would hang around the office until he fell asleep and Lincoln would take him off to the bedroom.

12. *His Character*

He seemed simple, yet he was complex. He spoke little, thought much. He read little, yet he knew much. He said once: "I am slow to learn and slow to forget that which I have learned. My mind is like a piece of steel—very hard to scratch anything on it, and almost impossible after you get it there, to rub it out." When he read something, he liked to read it aloud. Asked about this habit he replied: "I catch the idea by two senses for when I read aloud I hear what is read and I see it; and hence two senses get it and I remember it better, if I do not understand it better."

He was kind, magnanimous, self-controlled, humble. But he had no false modesty. Aware of his gifts, he was convinced of his own superiority. John Hay, who observed him for years, said that it would be absurd to call Lincoln a modest man. "No great man is ever modest. It was his intellectual arrogance and unconscious assumption of superiority that men like Chase and Sumner could never forgive."

Money had no undue influence on his life, though he was careful about it. When he died he left some $90,000, which under Judge David Davis's administration was increased to $110,974.62.

He was a poor administrator; there was no coordination between the executive departments. The relationship with Congress was as bad as it could be. He had not the gift to win the goodwill of politicians, who opposed him.

He had faith in the people, faith in the basic goodness of men, faith in democracy. He believed that "the people when rightly and fully trusted [will] return the trust." He said: "In leaving the people's business in their hands, we cannot go wrong." And he believed that "The people of these United States are the rightful masters of both Congress and Courts, not to overthrow the Constitution, but to overthrow the men who pervert the Constitution."

He tried to appeal to their reason, not to their emotions and prejudices. "And his appeal to the country at large," said Henry Croly, "was an appeal to its nobler side, its better nature." Once in a speech at Clinton he was supposed to have said (though there is no real proof that he really did say it): "You can fool some of the people all of the time and all of the people some of the time, but you cannot fool all of the people all of the time."

Many years before he became President he speculated: "The legitimate object of government is to do for a community of people whatever they need to have done, but can not do at all, or can not so well do for themselves, in their separate and individual capacities. In all that the people can individually do as well for themselves, government ought not to interfere."

He listened with patience to the stories of the long line of women—the wives and mothers of soldiers who came to him to ask promotions or beg pardons for their sons and husbands. Whenever he could, he helped. Whenever he could save a life, he would.

"Please have the adjutant general ascertain whether Second Lieutenant of Company D, 2nd Infantry, Alexander E. Drake is entitled to promotion. His wife thinks he is," read one of the notes to the Secretary of War. Another one: "To-day, Mrs. Major Paul of the Regular Army calls and urges the appointment of her husband as Brig.-Gen. She is a saucy woman and I am afraid she will keep tormenting me till I have to do it." Here is a communication to General Meade, sent a day after the Gettysburg address: "An intelligent woman [in] deep distress, called this morning, saying her husband, a Lieutenant in the A. P. was to be shot next Monday for desertion; and putting a letter in my hand, upon which I relied for particulars, she left without mentioning a name, or other particular by which to identify the case. . . . If you have a case which you shall think is probably the one intended, please apply my dispatch of this morning to it."

Some of his notes to Stanton bubble with humor. In one, revoking the sentences of soldiers who ran away from battle, Lincoln wrote: "It would frighten the poor fellows too terribly to kill them."

They also show how adamant he could be. Here is an exchange of notes between the President and his Secretary of War:

216

Dear Stanton:
Appoint this man a chaplain in the army.
                              A. Lincoln

Dear Mr. Lincoln:
He is not a preacher.
                              E. M. Stanton

Dear Stanton:
He is now.
                              A. Lincoln

Dear Mr. Lincoln:
There is no vacancy.
                              E. M. Stanton

Dear Stanton:
Appoint him chaplain-at-large.
                              A. Lincoln

Dear Mr. Lincoln:
There is no warrant in law for this.
                              E. M. Stanton

Dear Stanton:
Appoint him anyhow.
                              A. Lincoln

Dear Mr. Lincoln:
I will not.

                        E. M. Stanton

But Stanton did not always have the last word. When Lincoln told him: "I personally wish Jacob R. Freese, of New Jersey, to be appointed a Colonel for a colored regiment—and this regardless of whether he can tell the exact shade of Julius Caesar's hair," Freese had to be appointed.

He was free from personal animosity. He appointed men to high office, if he was convinced that it was in the best interests of the country, even if he knew that they were his personal enemies. He disliked quarrels. He said: "A man has not the time to spend half his life in quarrels. If any man ceases to attack me, I never remember the past against him."

He was humble, and was not worn down by the feeling of revenge. He said: "I am a patient man— always willing to forgive on the Christian terms of repentance, and also to give ample time for repentance." He advised one of his Generals: "I wish you to do nothing merely for revenge, but that what you may do shall be solely done with reference to the security of the future."

He seldom lost his composure. "If I do get up a little temper I have no sufficient time to keep it up," he wrote to General Sigel in 1863.

He had a capacity to grow. Horace Greeley told of him that "there was probably no year of his life when he was not a wiser, cooler and better man than he had been the year before."

His sympathy for those who lost loved ones in the war provoked deeply felt letters. To Fanny McCullough, daughter of Colonel Williams McCullough of the 4th Illinois Infantry, he wrote:

"Dear Fanny

It is with deep grief that I learn of the death of your kind and brave Father; and especially, that it is affecting your young heart beyond what is common in such cases. In this sad world of ours, sorrow comes to all; and, to the young, it comes with bitterest agony, because it takes them unawares. The older have learned to ever expect it. I am anxious to afford some alleviation of your present distress. Perfect relief is not possible, except with time. You can not now realize that you will ever feel better. Is not this so? And yet it is a mistake. You are sure to be happy again. To know this,

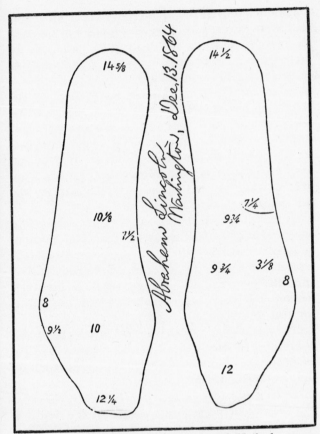

LINCOLN'S FEET, as outlined by himself. He had constant trouble with them, and had difficulty in getting the right shoes.

which is certainly true, will make you some less miserable now. I have had experience enough to know what I say; and you need only to believe it, to feel better at once. The memory of your dear Father, instead of an agony, will yet be a sad sweet feeling in your heart, of a purer, and holier sort than you have known before."

219

And to Lydia Bixby, a Boston widow, who supposedly lost five of her sons in the war, he sent these unforgettable lines:

"I feel how weak and fruitless must be any word of mine which should attempt to beguile you from the grief of a loss so overwhelming. But I cannot refrain from tendering to you the consolation that may be found in the thanks of the Republic they died to save.

"I pray that our Heavenly Father may assuage the anguish of your bereavement, and leave you only the cherished memory of the loved and lost, and the solemn pride that must be yours, to have laid so costly a sacrifice upon the altar of Freedom."

He was a religious man, though not a member of any organized church. He loved the Bible and knew it intimately. Once he told Noah Brooks: "I have been driven many times upon my knees by the overwhelming conviction that I had nowhere else to go. My own wisdom and that of all about me seemed insufficient for that day."

One day in late 1864 two ladies from Tennessee begged him for the release of their husbands, who were held prisoners of war. One of the ladies kept repeating that her husband was a religious man. The President ordered the release of the prisoners and said to the lady: "You say your husband is a religious man; tell him when you meet him, that I say I am not much judge of religion, but that, in my opinion, the religion that sets men to rebel and fight against their government, because, as they think, that government does not sufficiently help *some* men to eat their bread in the sweat of *other* men's faces, is not a sort of religion upon which people can get to heaven."

He loved to laugh. The painter Carpenter noted: "Mr. Lincoln's laugh stood by itself. The 'neigh' of a wild horse on his native prairie is not more undisguised and hearty." For Lincoln, laughter was a life preserver, laughter was—as he once described it—"the joyous, beautiful, universal evergreen of life." Without laughter he could not have lived.

His stories—and he had dozens of them ready— were always used to illuminate a point, to make a thought clearer, to clinch an argument. More often than not they began "That reminds me. . . ."

When someone asked him whether the harsh criticism of Horace Greeley disturbed him, Lincoln retorted: "It reminds me of the big fellow whose little wife beat him over the head without a resistance. When his friends remonstrated the man turned to them: 'Let her alone. It don't hurt me and it does her a power of good.'"

During the 1864 election he was asked to interfere openly in the fight between the two factions of the Republican party. But he thought it was wiser to stay out of it. "I learned a great many years ago that in a fight between husband and wife, a third party should never get between the woman's skillet and the man's ax-halve."

To John Hay's remark that, in his opinion, General Butler was the only man in the army in whose hands power would be dangerous, came the reply:

"Yes, he is like Jim Jett's brother. Jim used to say that his brother was the damndest scoundrel that ever lived, but in the infinite mercy of Providence he was also the damndest fool."

When a group of senators came to urge Lincoln to reorganize his Cabinet, the President was reminded of an old farmer back in Illinois who was pestered by skunks. One night the farmer went out with his shotgun, hid himself in a woodpile and waited. Before long there appeared not one skunk, but seven. He took aim and killed one, but that one raised such a fearful smell that he concluded it was best to let the other six go. There was no more talk that day about the reorganization of the Cabinet. The Senators took the hint, and they understood.

Lincoln never told a joke for the joke's sake; said his Secretary of State Seward, "they are like parables, lessons of wisdom."

An unusually savage attack in the New York *Tribune* reminded him of a backwoods traveler lost in a thunderstorm. Lightning streaked and thunder roared; the wrath of God was loose. After a terrible crash the traveler went to his knees, praying: "O, Lord, if it is all the same to you, give us a little more light and a little less noise!"

And the attacks of the Radical Republicans brought to his mind an old acquaintance who gave his son a microscope, and from that moment on, the boy looked at everything through the glass. One day at dinner his father took a piece of cheese. "Don't eat that, Father," cried the boy, "it is full of wrigglers." "My son," said the old man, biting into the cheese, "let them wriggle; I can stand it if they can."

He could joke about himself as easily as he could about other people. When someone inquired how it felt to be President of such a great country as the United States, he was reminded of what the tarred and feathered man said when his neighbors were riding him out of town on a rail. When asked how he liked it, he said that if it wasn't for the honor of the thing, he would much rather walk.

"They say I tell many stories," he said. "I reckon I do; but I have learned from long experience that *plain* people, take them as they run, are more easily *influenced* through the medium of a *broad* and humorous illustration than in any other way; and what the hypercritical *few* may think, I don't care."

222

13. *His Marriage*

Much has been written about his unhappy married life. But his marriage was no worse than others. Mary was not a shrew. She was a good wife and a good mother, who loved her husband and loved her children. They had their fights—what married couple has none? Mary's nerves were often frayed; she was sensitive, easily hurt by a careless word, and she had no sense of humor. But she was always true and loyal to her husband.

Her sense of values was not like his. When she first came to Washington she thought she could draw society into her orbit if she dressed well and gave glittering parties. Without Lincoln's knowledge Mary spent a great amount of money on clothes, running up a huge debt, a perpetual nightmare for many years to come.

Even if she had been different, she would not have been able to win the Washington ladies to her side. Those with Southern sympathies despised her because she had turned her back on the South, while those who

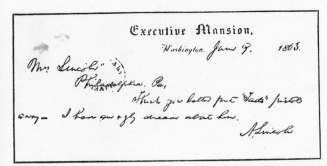

THE ANXIOUS LINCOLN wires his wife: "Think you better put 'Tad's' pistol away—I had an ugly dream about him."

upheld the Northern cause rumored that she was a Southern spy.

Mary was jealous of Lincoln, and he surreptitiously enjoyed it. Once while she was dressing for a reception their conversation was overheard by her seamstress, who recalled it.

"Well, Mother," asked Lincoln with a merry twinkle in his eyes. "Who must I talk with to-night—shall it be Mrs. D.?"

Mary took the bait. "That deceitful woman! No, you shall not listen to her flattery."

"Well, then, what do you say to Miss C.? She is too young and handsome to practice deceit."

"Young and handsome, you call her? You should not judge beauty for me. No, she is in the league with Mrs. D. and you shall not talk with her."

"Well, Mother, I must talk with someone. Is there any one that you do not object to?" he asked with a mock expression of gravity.

"I don't know as it is necessary that you should talk to any one in particular. You know well enough, Mr. Lincoln, that I do not approve of your flirtations with silly women, just as if you were a beardless boy, fresh from school."

"But, Mother, I insist that I must talk with somebody. I can't stand around like a simpleton, and say nothing. If you will not tell me who I may talk with, please tell me who I may *not* talk with."

"There is Mrs. D. and Miss C. in particular. I detest them both. Mrs. B. also will come around you, but you need not listen to her flattery. These are the ones in particular."

"Very well, Mother, now that we have settled the question to your satisfaction we will go downstairs."

If she imagined that a woman attracted her husband, she could not restrain herself. Her temper flared, as at a

THE BERRY-LINCOLN STORE in New Salem. It is probable that Ann Rutledge, Lincoln's legendary sweetheart, shopped there in 1832, as shown in this replica of the store.

HIGHLIGHTS OF HIS LIFE

THE CELEBRATED WRESTLING BOUT. Jack Armstrong, leader of the Clary's Grove boys, challenged Lincoln to a match, to which the whole village of New Salem turned out.

Painting by Harold von Schmidt for Esquire *Magazine*

HIS LAW OFFICE ON THE CIRCUIT was sometimes under a shady tree outside the courthouse. Here Lincoln consulted with local attorneys and listened to the stories of clients.

DEBATING WITH DOUGLAS at Charleston. In the senatorial contest of 1858 Lincoln was the candidate of the Republicans. He challenged Senator Douglas, his Democratic opponent, to a series of joint debates. Douglas accepted; a number of widely attended discussions on slavery followed.

HIS FIRST INAUGURATION. With James Buchanan, the outgoing President, Lincoln enters the Senate Chamber on March 4, 1861, to see Hamlin sworn in as Vice-President.

THE FIRST INAUGURAL. Before the unfinished Capitol, on a cold and blustery March day, Lincoln delivered a moderate and conciliatory inaugural address. He pleaded with the South: "We are not enemies, but friends. We must not be enemies. Though passion may have strained, it must not break our bonds of affection." A listener noted: "Old Abe delivered the greatest speech of the age . . . backbone all over."

READING THE EMANCIPATION PROCLAMATION to the Cabinet on Sept. 22, 1862. L. to r.: Stanton (War), Chase (Treasury), Lincoln, Welles (Navy), Seward (State), Smith (Interior), Blair (Postmaster Gen.), Bates (Attorney Gen.).

★

THE GETTYSBURG ADDRESS. Celebrities at the Gettysburg National Cemetery waiting for the beginning of the consecration ceremonies on Nov. 19, 1863. A recently found photograph purportedly showing President Lincoln (center).

THE SECOND INAUGURAL, March 4, 1865. Lincoln speaks the closing words of his immortal address: "With malice towards none; with charity for all; with firmness in the right, as God gives us to see the right, let us strive on to finish the work we are in." Few among the audience realize that they hear one of the greatest speeches of the age.

THE ASSASSINATION. On April 14, 1865, actor John Wilkes Booth shot the President in Ford's Theatre, while Lincoln listened to the comedy "Our American Cousin."

★

LINCOLN'S DEATH. At 7:22 the following morning the President breathed his last in a little room opposite the theatre. A voice said: "Now he belongs to the ages."

THE ASSASSIN
Twenty - six - year - old
John Wilkes Booth,
who killed Lincoln, was
shot twelve days later in
a Virginia barn where
he was hiding. In his
pocket were found the
pictures of five women.

THE END OF THE CONSPIRATORS. Mary G. Surratt, her
skirt tied with a rope; Lewis Payne, the attempted mur-
derer of Secretary of State Seward; David Herold and
George Atzerodt. The others received long prison terms.

troop inspection when she learned that General Ord's wife was riding alongside the President.

"What does this woman mean by riding by the side of the President and ahead of me? Does she suppose that *he* wants *her* by the side of him?" she asked in agitation. And when she caught up with the beautiful Mrs. Ord, she created a scene long to be remembered.

Most members of Mary's family remained with the South. Three of her half-brothers fighting for the Confederacy gave their lives; her favorite brother-in-law was killed in battle. Bent under her fate, Mary never wavered in her sympathies. She stood with her husband and with the North. She told her colored dressmaker: "Why should I sympathize with the rebels? Are they not against me? They would hang my husband to-morrow if it was in their power, and perhaps gibbet me with him. How then can I sympathize with a people at war with me and mine?"

Yet rumors made her out a disloyal person. When the mutterings went so far that a congressional investigation committee was ready to look into her loyalty, Lincoln walked up to the Capitol and testified: "I, Abraham Lincoln, President of the United States, appear of my own volition before this Committee of the Senate to say that I, of my own knowledge, know that it is untrue that any of my family hold treasonable communication with the enemy."

Mary, like many spirited and intelligent women, could not resist meddling in her husband's affairs. She had strong and definite opinions.

On one occasion she told him:

"Father, you are too honest for this world! You should have been born a saint. You will generally find it a safe rule to distrust a disappointed, ambitious politician. It makes me mad to see you sit still and let that hypocrite Seward, twine you around his finger as if you were a skein of thread." Of Chase she had an equally low opinion. "If he thought he could make anything by it, he would betray you to-morrow." General McClellan was for her a "humbug," who "talks too much and does so little." General Grant was "an obstinate fool and a butcher."

Lincoln retorted with some irony: "Well, Mother, supposing that we give you command of the army. No doubt you would do much better than any general that has been tried."

But they loved each other with tenderness and great affection. If she was away from Washington, he was longing for her. "The air is so clear and cool, and apparently healthy," he wired her, "that I would be glad for you to come." And a day later he urged her: "I really wish to see you." During their twenty-two years of married life there was never a morsel of gossip that he sought the company of other women. His feel-

A LONGING WIRE TO MARY when she was away from home. Lincoln tells her: "The air is so clear and cool, and apparently healthy, that I would be glad for you to come. Nothing very particular, but I would be glad to see you ..."

ing for her is best summed up in his own words. At a reception in the White House a correspondent of the *Christian Register* was standing next the President while Mary was chatting with some guests. Lincoln looked at her in admiration. "My wife is as handsome," he said, "as when she was a girl and I a poor nobody then fell in love with her, and what is more, I have never fallen out."

14. *The Final Battles*

The time of the Confederacy was running out. In the middle of December 1864 the Southern invasion of Tennessee was repulsed: General Thomas defeated his adversary at Nashville so completely that the Confederate army in the West never recovered.

On December 10, General Sherman set out from Atlanta. As his men marched through Georgia, living on the land, cutting a swath of devastation sixty miles wide, they made the state "an example to rebels." Sherman brought the frightfulness of the conflict to the South. Gone was the gentlemanly war; war was hell. Less than two weeks later his troops reached the sea; Georgia was cut in two. On December 22, Sherman wired to Lincoln: "I beg to present you as a Christmas gift the city of Savannah, with 150 heavy guns and plenty of ammunition; also about 25,000 bales of cotton."

Hope and joy rose in the North. In thanking Sherman for the victory Lincoln admitted that when the General left Atlanta for the Atlantic coast, "I was anxious, if not fearful; but feeling that you were the better judge, and remembering that 'nothing risked, nothing gained,' I did not interfere. Now, the undertaking being a success, the honor is all yours; for I believe none of us went further than to acquiesce.

And taking the work of Gen. Thomas into the count, as it should be taken, it is indeed a great success."

To the military victories came political ones. Lincoln's re-election implied a mandate for the reintroduction of the Thirteenth Amendment, prohibiting slavery and involuntary servitude within the confines of the United States. The amendment had previously failed to pass in the House of Representatives; in his annual message to Congress the President asked that it be reconsidered.

The United States was on its way to become a free nation. Slavery was dying; even before the Thirteenth Amendment was passed at the end of January 1865, Arkansas, Louisiana, Maryland and Missouri had abolished it; and Tennessee and Kentucky were willing to follow suit.

Early in January 1865, Francis Preston Blair, Andrew Jackson's friend and member of his Kitchen Cabinet, journeyed to Richmond to sound out Jefferson Davis about peace. Davis was ready to negotiate with the North so peace could return "to the two countries." But when Blair delivered this message, Lincoln corrected Davis: the North would parley with the South so that peace could return "to the people of our one common country."

Thus, on the third day of February the President, accompanied by William H. Seward, his Secretary of State, met with the three appointed Confederate negotiators—Alexander H. Stephens, the Vice-President of the Confederacy, R. M. T. Hunter, and Judge John A. Campbell—on board the transport *River Queen* at Hampton Roads. The five men conferred for many hours. Lincoln told the commissioners that he still believed in compensated emancipation. If hostilities would cease, he would propose to set $400,000,000 aside to indemnify the owners of slaves. But until the rebellious states would lay down their arms, he would not bargain with them. One of the Confederate commissioners retorted that even King Charles I had parleyed with the men who took up arms against his government, to which Lincoln replied with a quizzical smile that, though he was not too well posted in history, he distinctly remembered that Charles had lost his head.

Hunter spoke up: "Mr. President, if we understand you correctly, you think that we of the Confederacy have committed treason; that we are traitors to our government; that we have forfeited our rights, and are proper subjects for the hangman. Is not that about what your words imply?"

"Yes," rejoined Lincoln, "you have stated the proposition better than I did. That is about the size of it."

After a pregnant pause Hunter said pleasantly: "Well, Mr. Lincoln, we have about concluded that we shall not be hanged as long as you are President—if we behave ourselves."

The talk ended amicably but without political results. Seward sent a basket of champagne after the commissioners by a Negro in a rowboat. Through the boatswain's megaphone the Secretary of State's voice sounded over the water. "Keep the champagne," bellowed Seward, then added with a chuckle, "but return the Negro!"

The war went on, the destruction went on, and men had to suffer and men had to die. It seemed so senseless, now that the end was so clear.

A month after his talk at Hampton Roads, Lincoln was inaugurated for the second time. March 4 turned out to be a somber and drizzly day, the roads covered with mud, a cold and gusty wind blowing. As he appeared at the inaugural stand, a tremendous cheer greeted him. And when it had subsided, he spoke:

At this second appearing to take the oath of the presidential office, there is less occasion for an extended address than there was at the first. Then a statement, somewhat in detail, of a course to be pursued, seemed fitting and proper. Now, at the expiration of four years, during which public declarations have been constantly called forth on every point and phase of the great contest which still absorbs the attention, and engrosses the energies of the nation, little that is new could be presented. The progress of our arms, upon which all else chiefly depends, is as well known to the public as to myself; and it is, I trust, reasonably satisfactory and encouraging to all. With high hope for the future, no prediction in regard to it is ventured.

On the occasion corresponding to this four years ago, all thoughts were anxiously directed to an impending civil war. All dreaded it—all sought to avert it. While the inaugeral address was being delivered from this place, devoted altogether to saving the Union without war, insurgent agents were in

THE SECOND INAUGURAL. The final script of the address was written out by the President on four foolscap pages.

the city seeking to destroy it without war seeking to dissolve the Union, and divide effects, by negotiation. Both parties deprecated war; but one of them would make war rather than let the nation survive; and the other would accept war rather than let it perish. And the war came.

One eighth of the whole population were colored slaves, not distributed generally over the Union, but localized in the Southern part of it. These slaves constituted a peculiar and powerful interest. All knew that this interest was, somehow, the cause of the war. To strengthen, perpetuate, and extend this interest was the object for which the insurgents would rend the Union, even by war; while the government claimed no right to do more than to restrict the territorial enlargement of it. Neither party expected for the war, the magnitude, or the duration, which it has already attained. Neither anticipated that

THE FACSIMILE OF THE SECOND PAGE of the inaugural. Lincoln did not read his speech from this manuscript, but

the cause of the conflict might cease with, or even before, the conflict itself should cease, Each looked for an easier triumph, and a result less fundamental and astounding. Both read the same Bible, and pray to the same God; and each invokes His aid against the other. It may seem strange that any men should dare to ask a just God's assistance in wringing their bread from the sweat of other men's faces; but let us judge not that we be not judged. The prayers of both could not be answered; that of neither has been answered fully. The Almighty has His own purposes. "Woe unto the world because of offences! for it must needs be that offences come; but woe to that man by whom the offence cometh!" If we shall suppose that American Slavery is one of those offences which, in the providence of God, must needs come, but which, having continued through His appointed time, He now wills to remove, and that He gives to both North and South, this terrible war, as the woe due to those

from a printed galley which a Washington newspaper compositor obligingly set in two broad columns on a single sheet.

by whom the offence came, shall we discern there
in any departure from those divine attributes
which the believers in a Living God always
ascribe to Him? Fondly do we hope— fervent
ly do we pray— that this mighty scourge of
war may speedily pass away. Yet, if God
wills that it continue, until all the wealth
piled by the bond-man's two hundred and
fifty years of unrequited toil shall be sunk,
and until every drop of blood drawn with the
lash, shall be paid by another drawn with
the sword, as was said three thousand years
ago, so still it must be said "the judgments
of the Lord, are true and righteous altogether"

With malice toward none;
with charity for all; with firmness in the
right, as God gives us to see the right,
let us strive on to finish the work we
are in; to bind up the nation's wounds;
to care for him who shall have borne the battle, and for his widow, and his orphan—
to do all which may achieve and cherish a just,
and a lasting peace, among ourselves, and with all nations.

THE FOURTH PAGE of the second inaugural address, containing that immortal last paragraph, perhaps Lincoln's best.

Later in March, General Grant asked the President to visit his headquarters, as he would like to talk with him, besides, "the rest would do you good." Lincoln boarded the *River Queen*, and with Mary and Tad sailed for City Point.

General Sherman arrived from North Carolina, and on the evening of the twenty-seventh the President met with Grant, Sherman and Admiral Porter in the cabin of his boat for a discussion. Their conference lasted till late into the night, and the next day it was continued. They talked about the terms of surrender and the future of the South. Lincoln desired—once the rebel forces had laid down their arms—to guarantee the men in the South all the rights as citizens of a common country, and he spoke out the hope that a final bloody battle could be avoided. "There had been enough blood shed."

Grant left City Point to direct the final assault against

AN ARTIST'S CONCEPTION OF THE INAUGURAL BALL

AT CITY POINT. A sketch from life, drawn by Albert Hunt on March 27, 1865, during a visit with General Grant.

the Confederacy. From the field he sent some battle flags to the President, and Lincoln rejoiced: "Here is something material, something I can see, feel and understand. This means victory. This *is* victory."

The end was in sight. On April 3 Union troops took Richmond. The Confederate capital, the symbol of Confederate strength, surrendered.

Next day a happy Lincoln left for that city. As he drove through its streets, Negroes crowded around him, knelt before him. "You must kneel to God only and thank Him for your freedom," he told them. A colored man cried out: "Bress de Lawd, dere is de great Messiah!" The President smiled. To an observer he looked "pale, and haggard, utterly worn out." That evening when General Weitzel asked him how to treat the conquered people, the President replied: "If I were in your place, I'd let 'em up easy, let 'em up easy."

On April 6 Grant relayed Sheridan's message to the President, reporting the capture of seven thousand prisoners and a great amount of war equipment. Sheridan advised: "If the thing is pressed I think that Lee will surrender." And Lincoln wired back: "Let the *thing* be pressed."

Lee's supply lines had been cut, his troops were outnumbered by five to one. His men were without shoes, they were lacking ammunition.

On April 8 the President was on his way to Washington. On that day Grant exchanged notes with Lee.

Head Quarters Armies of the United States,
City Point, April 7. 11. Am 1865

Lieut Gen. Grant.

Gen. Sheridan says "If the thing is pressed I think that Lee will surrender." Let the ~~thing~~ be pressed.

A. Lincoln

ON APRIL 6, 1865, three days before Appomattox, Grant sent Lincoln a message from General Sheridan in which Sheridan said: "If the thing is pressed I think that Lee will surrender." The President replied with the above dispatch.

"DAR COME MARSE LINKUM, de Sabior ob the lan'—we so glad to see him," came the greeting from a colored man as the unattended President drove into the former Confederate capital on April 4, 1865, after Richmond's surrender.

Next morning Lincoln visited Secretary Seward, who had been seriously injured in a carriage accident. Seward, his face and neck in bandages, whispered: "You are back from Richmond?" "Yes," came the reply, "and I think we are near the end at last."

About the time Lincoln made his visit General Lee surrendered to Grant at Appomattox Court House.

The following night a cheering crowd came to the Executive Mansion in Washington and asked for the President. Lincoln spoke, thoughtful and sober, pondering over the future of the rebellious states.

"We all agree that the seceded States, so called, are

245

out of their practical relation with the Union; and that the sole object of the Government, civil and military, in regard to those States is to again get them into that proper practical relation. I believe it is not only possible, but in fact, easier to do this, without deciding, or even considering whether these States have ever been out of the Union, than with it. Finding themselves safely at home, it would be utterly immaterial whether they had ever been abroad. Let us all join in doing the acts necessary to restoring the proper practical relations between these States and the Union; and each forever after, innocently indulge his own opinion whether, in doing the acts, he brought the States from without, into the Union, or only gave them proper assistance, they never having been out of it."

Tad stood next to his father as he spoke, and he heard the oration of Senator Harlan, who asked emotionally, "What shall we do with the rebels?"

As the crowd shouted: "Hang them," Tad—so the story goes—turned to his father: "No, no, papa. Not hang them. Hang on to them!" "That's it," cried out Lincoln. "Tad has got it. We must hang onto them!"

15. *An Ominous Dream*

One night in April, Lincoln had a strange dream and he spoke about it to Mary.

"About ten days ago," he told her, "I retired very late. I had been up waiting for important dispatches from the front. I could not have been long in bed when I fell into a slumber, for I was weary. I soon began to dream. There seemed to be a deathlike stillness about me. Then I heard subdued sobs, as if a number of people were weeping. I thought I left my bed and wandered downstairs. Here the silence was broken by the same pitiful sobbing, but the mourners were invisible.

I went from room to room; no living person was in sight, but the same mournful sounds of distress met me as I passed along. I saw light in all the rooms; every object was familiar to me; but where were all the people who were grieving as if their hearts would break? I was puzzled and alarmed. What could be the meaning of all this? Determined to find the cause of a state of things so mysterious and so shocking, I kept on until I arrived at the East Room, which I entered. There I met with a sickening surprise. Before me was a catafalque, on which rested a corpse wrapped in funeral vestments. Around it were stationed soldiers who were acting as guards; and there was a throng of people, gazing mournfully upon the corpse, whose face was covered, others weeping pitifully. 'Who is dead in the White House?' I demanded of one of the soldiers. 'The President,' was his answer; 'he was killed by an assassin.' Then came a loud burst of grief from the crowd, which awoke me from my dreams. I slept no more that night; and although it was only a dream, I have been strangely annoyed by it ever since."

The dream upset Mary. "I wish you had not told it. I am glad I don't believe in dreams, or I should be in terror from this time forth."

"Well, it is only a dream, Mary. Let us say no more about it, and try to forget it."

But how could she forget it? She had heard of letters coming with every mail, letters of warning, letters of threat. She had dark premonitions. But when he was warned, when his best friends implored him not to leave the mansion without a guard and never to stroll alone on the streets, he only laughed.

"What does anybody want to assassinate me for?" he asked. "If anyone wants to do so, he can do it any day or night, if he is ready to give his life for mine. It is nonsense."

247

To Ward Hill Lamon he said about his dream: "Hill, your apprehension of harm to me from some hidden enemy is downright foolishness. For a long time you have been trying to keep somebody—the Lord knows who—from killing me. Don't you see how it will turn out? In this dream it was not me, but some other fellow, that was killed. It seems that the ghostly assassin tried his hand on some one else. And this reminds me of an old farmer in Illinois whose family were made sick by eating greens. Some poisonous herb got into the mess, and members of the family were in danger of dying. There was a half-witted boy in the family called Jake; and always afterward when they had greens the old man would say, 'Now, afore we risk these greens, let's try 'em on Jake. If he stands 'em, we're all right.' Just so with me. As long as this imaginary assassin continues to exercise himself on others *I* can stand it."

16. *His Last Day*

On April 14 General Anderson hoisted again the flag of the Union at Fort Sumter; on that day the Secretary of War proclaimed that further drafts and recruiting would be suspended, and on that day Lincoln wrote to General Van Alen, expressing the hope that the restored Union would become "a Union of hearts and hands as well as of States."

To John A. J. Creswell, who came to see him, the President said: "Creswell, old fellow, everything is bright this morning. The war is over. . . . We are going to have good times now, and a united country."

On that morning a Cabinet meeting was held, to which General Grant was invited to attend. The restoration and re-establishment of the Union was discussed. Who should be recognized as state authority? Lincoln said: "We can't undertake to run State governments in all these Southern States. Their people must do that—though I reckon that at first some of them may do it badly." And what should be the fate of the Confederate leaders? There was some speculation whether they would flee or whether they would allow themselves to be captured and tried. Postmaster General Dennison asked: "I suppose, Mr. President, you would not be sorry to have them escape out of the country?"

"Well," came the answer, "I should not be sorry to have them out of the country; but I should be for following them up pretty close, to make sure of their going."

General Grant reported on Lee's surrender and his terms to the Confederate soldiers. "I told them to go back to their homes and families, and they would not be molested, if they did nothing more." Lincoln nodded in agreement. The President then spoke of members in Congress "who possess feelings of hate and vindictiveness in which I do not sympathize and can not participate."

The Cabinet meeting over, Lincoln saw some more visitors. He received Nancy Bushrod, a colored woman who had come to petition for her soldier husband's pay. "My good woman, perhaps you'll see many a day when all the food in the house is a single loaf of bread. Even so, give every child a slice and send your children off to school." With that he bowed before Nancy—and she never forgot it—"lak I wuz a natchral bawn lady."

Then he signed the pardon of a deserter, commenting: "Well, I think the boy can do us more good above ground than under ground."

In the afternoon, as was his habit, he drove out with Mary. In a happy mood he daydreamed about the future.

"We have had a hard time since we came to Washington," he said to her, "but the war is over, and with God's blessing, we may hope for four years of peace and happiness, and then we will go back to Illinois and pass the rest of our lives in quiet. We have laid by some money, and during this time, we will save up more, but shall not have enough to support us. We will go back to Illinois. I will open a law office at Springfield or Chicago and practice law, and at least do enough to help give us a livelihood."

Returning from the drive, he was not in the mood to work. To Governor Oglesby of Illinois and General Haynie, who came for a visit, he read a few chapters of Petroleum V. Nasby's *Letters* with such abandon and pleasure that dinner had to wait.

After his meal he walked over to the War Department to see whether any news had come from Sherman's army. Then it was time to go to the theatre. In the morning it had been planned that the President and Mrs. Lincoln would visit Ford's Theatre to see "Our American Cousin," and General Grant and his wife were to go with them. The capital was crowded with soldiers and officers, all eager to see the President and the chief of the army. Grant, however, anxious to leave Washington, asked to be excused, so Mrs. Lincoln invited Miss Clara Harris and Major Henry Reed Rathbone, the daughter and stepson of Senator Ira Harris.

The presidential party reached the theatre when the show was already in progress. As the President entered, the actors ceased playing, and the band struck up "Hail to the Chief." Lincoln bowed to the audience, then took a seat in the rocking chair at the back of the box.

And while he watched the play, a young man went on with the mad design to kill him. Twenty-six-year-old John Wilkes Booth, a member of the famous theatrical family, a romantic lover of the South, his mind

THE SCENE AT FORD'S THEATRE

WHERE LINCOLN WAS MURDERED. A contemporary sketch of the box in Ford's Theatre, drawn by A. R. Waud.

AFTER THE ASSASSINATION, Booth leaped to the stage, shouting, "Sic semper tyrannis" (ever thus to tyrants).

TWO CONTEMPORARY DRAWINGS OF THE SCENES AFTER LINCOLN'S ASSASSINATION

OUTSIDE THE STAGE DOOR a chore boy waited for Booth, who jumped on the horse and galloped away.

THE FATALLY WOUNDED PRESIDENT was carried from the theatre across Tenth Street to the Peterson House.

unbalanced and under the influence of alcohol, made his preparations with great care. A few hours before the play began, he was in the theatre boring a small hole in the door of the presidential box. Now he was back again—and as the guard had wandered away, no one interfered with him. For a few moments he looked through the spy hole. A little while before, Lincoln had reached out for Mary's hand and Mary whispered: "What will Miss Harris think?" And the President had laughed: "She won't think anything about it." He kept Mary's hand in his as he sat and enjoyed the comedy.

Quietly Booth entered the box. The interloper, in his right hand a small derringer, in his left a dagger, aimed his pistol at the President's head and pulled the trigger.

FROM OUR SPECIAL WAR CORRESPONDENT.
"CITY POINT, VA., *April* —, 8.30 A.M.
"All seems well with us."—A. LINCOLN.

THE LAST CARICATURE OF LINCOLN, drawn by Nast appeared in *Harper's Weekly* the day of his assassination.

THE ASSASSIN IN HIDING. When Booth stubbornly refused to surrender, the barn where he hid was set afire.

SHOT IN A BARN at Garrett's farm near Port Royal, Virginia, Booth was still alive when soldiers dragged him out.

LINCOLN'S FIRST BURIAL PLACE IN SPRINGFIELD

Lincoln slumped in his seat. Major Rathbone threw himself at the intruder. Booth wounded him with his dagger, then jumped over the box railing to the stage, eleven feet below. The spur of his riding boot caught in the flag which draped the box; he fell, but quickly was up and shouted: "*Sic semper tyrannis*" (ever thus to tyrants), the line of Brutus when he killed Caesar.

Pandemonium broke loose. A young army surgeon climbed into the presidential box. Mary clutched his arm. "Oh, Doctor! Is he dead?" Twenty-three-year-old Dr. Charles Leale looked at Lincoln's injury and his face darkened. The bullet had hit at the back of the President's head, crossed the brain and lodged itself behind the right eye. There was no hope.

The fatally wounded President was taken by his shoulders and legs and carried across the street to the nearest house, where he was laid on a bed.

Members of the Cabinet came, and high military officers. The Secretary of the Navy, who was present, noted in his diary: "The quaint sufferer lay extended diagonally across the bed, which was not long enough for him. He had been stripped of his clothes. His large arms, which were occasionally exposed, were of a size which one would scarce have expected from his spare appearance. His slow, full respiration lifted the clothes with each breath he took. His features were calm and striking."

During the night Lincoln fought with death. At 7:22 in the morning it was all over. The great and good man was at peace with the world.

"O Captain! my Captain! our fearful trip is done,
The ship has weather'd every rock, the prize we sought
    is won."

And in the stillness of the little room a voice was heard to say: "Now he belongs to the ages."

BRITTANIA MOURNS LINCOLN. The London *Punch*, which during the war was critical of the President's actions, printed this cartoon shortly after Lincoln's death.